REASON AND
RELIGIOUS FAITH

REASON AND RELIGIOUS FAITH

TERENCE PENELHUM
UNIVERSITY OF CALGARY

WestviewPress

A Division of HarperCollins*Publishers*

Focus Series

Copyright ©1995 by Westview Press, Inc., A Division of HarperCollins Publishers, Inc.

Published in 1995 in the United States of America by Westview Press, Inc., 5500 Central Avenue, Boulder, Colorado 80301-2877, and in the United Kingdom by Westview Press, 12 Hid's Copse Road, Cumnor Hill, Oxford OX2 9JJ

Library of Congress Cataloging-in-Publication Data
Penelhum, Terence, 1929–
    Reason and religious faith / Terence Penelhum.
        p.   cm. — (Focus series)
    Includes bibliograghical references and index.
    ISBN 0-8133-2035-6 (hc). — ISBN 0-8133-2036-4 (pbk.)
    1. Religion—Philosophy.   2. Faith.   3. Faith and reason.
I. Title.   II. Series: Focus series (Westview Press)
BL51.P3449   1995
210—dc20   95-2902
                                                                            CIP

The paper used in this publication meets the requirements of the American National Standard for Permanence of Paper for Printed Library Materials Z39.48-1984.

10   9   8   7   6   5   4   3   2   1

To Edith

CONTENTS

PREFACE

This book is intended to clarify and explore some of the special problems that religious faith raises for philosophy. But it is written in the conviction that these problems are of interest and importance not only to philosophers but also to serious students of religion and to theologians. In the first, introductory chapter I discuss why faith generates special philosophical perplexities. Since many of the problems that faith raises have been dealt with by major classical thinkers, whose opinions form the background of many important present-day discussions, in Chapter 2 I offer a highly condensed and selective account of some of the most important classical positions. Readers for whom this chapter is a mere repetition of the familiar are invited to pass over it and to look back later if references to some of those thinkers suggest that I have not understood them correctly.

Chapters 3 to 6 deal with what seems to me to be the central intellectual difficulty that faith presents: that is, the relation of faith to reason, or, alternatively, the epistemology of faith. But I have been anxious throughout to avoid being constrained either by traditional restrictions on the understanding of these phrases or by the limits imposed by currently fashionable attempts to break free of them. And even though I have at no time tried to conceal my own views, my main concern has been to elucidate the nature of the problems themselves; hence the frequency with which I may admit not knowing the answers.

I want here to acknowledge a number of debts. I am grateful to Hugo Meynell for many discussions of issues dealt with here and to our colleagues Eliezer Segal and Andrew Rippin for helpful suggestions. I want to thank Spencer Carr for his invitation to write this book and for his help and patience while I have been responding. Two anonymous readers who saw the product in an earlier version made valuable suggestions that have helped me remove many flaws. Special thanks, however, must go to Robert McKim, who read the whole manuscript with great care and sympathy and responded to both major and minor points with wisdom and insight. No one has ever done me a philosophical kindness to compare with this.

To my wife goes the sort of gratitude that belongs to someone to whose spiritual sustenance I owe anything worthwhile I could have to say on these themes and any others.

Terence Penelhum

CHAPTER ONE

Introduction

Faith and the Philosophy of Religion

Students of philosophy are familiar enough with the philosophy of religion and usually encounter it in one or more of three ways:

1. They may consider religious ideas as presenting special problems in conceptual analysis: Is it coherent, for example, to suppose we are created by a being who is all powerful, incorporeal, present everywhere, yet personal or to blame our sins on ourselves while ascribing any merits we may have to the grace of God?
2. Even if students judge religious doctrines to be coherent, they may still see them as very ambitious cosmic or metaphysical claims and ask whether they can possibly be proved or disproved: Can it be proved, most obviously, that God exists or that he does not?
3. Such questions force students to ask how far religious beliefs strain the limits of our capacities to attain truth or live according to reason: Is it rational to center one's life on beliefs about God and our supposed relationship to him, or are such beliefs arbitrary or even pathological?

The philosophical problems that are generated by faith are, for the most part, in the last of these three categories. Consequently, the philosophical study of faith has largely consisted of explorations in the epistemology of religion. In modern times these have been undertaken in contexts that have involved comparing the convictions of those who have faith with the convictions we all have outside religious contexts when we form commonsense beliefs, such as those that depend on the senses, or when we acquire scientific beliefs like those of astronomy or biology.

Faith and the "Study of Religion"

Students of religion, at least in nonsectarian institutions, are likely to examine religious traditions in a manner that is said to be phenomenological.[1] The purpose of the academic study of religion is thought to be that of understanding the beliefs and practices that can be discerned in these traditions rather than that of deciding on the truth of the claims they make. It is easy to suppose that such an enterprise does not require us to consider the sorts of questions that interest philosophers since these have to be put to one side in the interests of objectivity and fairness. But this supposition is unrealistic, not because the interest in religion that prompts the study of it may well come from personal involvement, even though that is sometimes true, but because the suspension of judgment that an objective study of religion requires does not exempt the student from confronting many other questions that are certainly philosophical. Three examples are enough to show this.

First, the major religious traditions of the world all have divisions and internal controversies. To understand these, it is essential to identify the bases on which those on one side of such internal divisions distinguish themselves from those on the other. To do so requires an understanding of how each side settles questions of religious authority, doctrine, or scriptural canon. We can understand such controversies without taking sides, but not without identifying the competing claims and standards involved. Such identification is a philosophical task, indeed an epistemological one. (It can be excluded from epistemology only if the latter is restricted to the activity of passing judgment on claims that someone else has identified. This restriction, as we see later, is a very dated one.) Second, all the major religions of the world make practical demands on their adherents that are, or appear to be, based on claims about our place in the cosmos and our need to work out our destiny in it. The relationship between those knowledge claims and the practical demands the traditions make on their members' conduct is fundamental to each tradition. But this relationship is not the same in each case; nor is an understanding of it something that can be arrived at without religious or scholarly controversy. Here again we confront a question that is often philosophical in nature: What is the relation between knowledge and moral practice? Third, and perhaps most important, as scholarly awareness of the details of the world's religious traditions is broadened and deepened, questions arise about their relationship to one another.

These questions do get attention within the religions themselves as each looks at the others, and the answers are very different: Hinduism is more obviously accommodating to what is said in other religious traditions than is Islam or Christianity, for example. But these questions have also been addressed by scholars of religion from a more general perspective; some of them want to know whether the divergencies between the religions are really as deep as they seem or whether they are culturally determined differences that can be judged to represent alternative responses to one reality. If this is not a philosophical question, it is hard to know what is. Obviously, anyone seeking to answer it has to confront all the major epistemological questions about the powers and limits of the human mind that interest, equally, the philosopher of perception and the metaphysician.[2]

These examples show that the academic study of the world's religions is not free of philosophy merely because those who engage in it may refrain from making judgments of each religion's truth. But that does not show that the philosophical questions to which the contemporary student of religion should attend are confined to the traditional Western philosophical concerns with the relation of faith to reason. That is because faith and religiousness cannot be identified.

"Faith" and "Religion"

The concept of faith seems to be much more restricted than that of religion. Faith is one of the states or attitudes demanded of the religious person and then, it seems, only in some of the major religions: namely, Judaism, Christianity, and Islam. It may indeed be that faith is also essential to Hinduism or Buddhism, which may be what causes some to refer to all the religions as "faiths." But whether they all require faith is an issue that needs discussion—

here is one more philosophical question that religion poses for us. I attempt to say a few sketchy things about this matter much later. For the moment I rest on the obvious appearances and say that faith is one attitude or state of mind that is characteristic of religious persons in some traditions, though it is not the whole of what those traditions demand of adherents or the whole of what they aspire to. Faith has attracted more philosophical attention than many other aspects of the religious life because it raises questions that exercise the philosophical mind independently: questions about the limits of human knowledge and the demands of reason. But the very fact that at least some great religious traditions require faith, and that it does raise these questions, shows that it is necessary for the student of religion as well as the philosopher to know about them. The serious study of the nature of any of these traditions requires us to contend with these questions, at least indirectly.

Theology

A similar involvement with philosophy falls to the lot of the student of theology. This book is not a theological work. But the questions it deals with are questions that the theologian confronts continually. Much theology is a philosophical activity that is carried on *within* faith: It is the activity of articulating what faith entails. Christian theologians, for example, do not (for the most part) debate between themselves whether God exists or whether Jesus is the son of God; but they do assume that only those who accept that these are truths can engage in Christian theology. But those who do engage in it may well find themselves debating whether God's reality can be known through natural reason or only through revelation, and they may well find themselves debating what, in detail, it *means* to say that Jesus was the son of God. The motives and premises of theology and the philosophy of religion are undoubtedly different, but the questions they ask are frequently the same. This book does not assume the faith commitment that the theologian assumes, but it does deal with questions that the theological student must explore.

Faith as a Phenomenon

Let us then begin, as philosophers and students of religion, to ask what problems faith presents. To do so, we have to be able to recognize examples of faith; that is, to be able, at least in a rough-and-ready way, to know who has faith and who does not. Deciding that faith is present, either in ourselves or in others, is not necessarily a straight-forward matter, but it does look as though we can be uncertain whether some people have faith only if we are clear in our minds that we could recognize others who do. But even here, at the very outset of inquiries into the nature and status of religious faith, we run into a difficulty: There are some very important accounts of faith that seem to say no one can identify it without having it or, at least, without accepting as true what the faithful person believes.

Two such views are those we find in Aquinas and in Pascal, whose opinions have been extremely influential.[3] Aquinas holds that faith is one of the theological virtues, which he defines as virtues that God implants within us. One is not able to accept this account of faith without having previously accepted that God exists and intervenes in human affairs. Pascal says that faith is God known by the heart and not by the reason. One cannot, similarly, accept this view of faith without believing in God. This might not seem to matter at first sight. After all, it is quite easy to say, for example, what the philosophical problems about miracles are regardless of whether one believes there are any. Why is the case of faith different? But the question only has to be put to answer itself: If Aquinas or Pascal is right, then someone who does not believe in God is forced to deny that there are any examples of faith to be found, just as such a person has to deny that any miracles ever happen. This position may seem plausible enough with regard to miracles, but it seems an absurd consequence to accept about faith.

Perhaps it is not really absurd. Many Jews, Christians, or Muslims might be quite willing to say that in the end only God knows which of his creatures truly have the faith they profess. But it certainly collides with the natural assumption that both sides make in the common debates about faith and reason: that many people indeed have faith and that the problem is to decide whether they should. I proceed here in the following way: I take for granted that the word *faith* is the name of a state of mind and of personality that exists and is characteristic of followers of at least some of the major religions of the world. The task of the philosophical student is to understand what is meant when we say someone has faith and to consider questions about its rationality and relationship to our human capacities to discover truth. Theological questions about whether human beings can bring about faith in themselves, how far it is necessary or sufficient for salvation, and the like I take to be questions that believers raise about the origin and implications of a state of the personality that believers and unbelievers alike can recognize to exist. If this assumption needs to be defended, I do so by pointing out that within some of the key scriptures of these religions individuals are identified as having faith and that the key formative personalities of these religions, such as Moses or Saint Paul, are surely paradigmatic examples of it.[4] For the remainder of this introduction, I try to indicate why faith is an object of puzzlement and even suspicion for philosophers and why a state of mind that has these puzzling features is still so central to the religious traditions in which it is demanded.

Why Faith Is Puzzling

Let us look at the puzzlement of philosophers first. For the most part they take for granted that faith is something found only within religion. As it is found there, faith seems to combine features that the practice of philosophy demands that a rational being keep apart. These are a wholehearted belief, on the one hand, and a recognized absence of conclusive evidence for it, on the other. To many philosophers it is not obvious that one *can* wholeheartedly believe anything that one does not think one has conclusive reasons to believe; and it is obvious to them that even if one can do this, one ought not to. We all know that many people believe things that they lack sufficient grounds for; but it is the task of philosophical thought to put them on their guard against doing so as far as possible. Yet not only does faith appear to combine these things; it also seems to make a virtue of the combination. The faithful (believers, as they are called) are commended for their apparent certainty in the face of what looks like counterevidence and are censured for having doubts in circumstances that would seem to make such doubts very reasonable. In nonreligious contexts we praise people for adjusting the strength of their beliefs to the quality of the evidence they have, but in religious contexts we find them being praised for ignoring defects in the evidence and persisting in spite of them. If we look at the reasons given for this praise, we find that they relate to religious teachings about salvation: that those who have faith are said to have achieved something that helps ensure their salvation and that those who do not are imperiling it. But this reasoning suggests that not only does faith make those who have it cling to beliefs that they do not have good reasons to hold, but also that they consciously do this because they hope to gain by it and are afraid of the consequences of changing their minds. Faith, then, seems to involve either wishful thinking or self-deception.

This problem about faith is familiar to anyone who has ever thought about it. Some philosophers have noticed that articulation of this problem leads immediately to another puzzle that faces both those who defend faith and those who attack it: To say that one ought to hold on to this or that belief in the face of difficult circumstances, or that one ought to give it up in the face of contradictory evidence, implies that one has control over what beliefs one holds. At least on the surface believers praise one another for freely doing something that their critics fault them for doing. How can either attitude be the right one unless beliefs (or at least *these* beliefs) can be freely taken on, sustained, or abandoned? But are beliefs matters of free choice? For all the centrality of the discussions of belief and knowledge in Western philosophical history, there has not been a great deal of attention to this issue. There are, however, a number of classic theories about it, and we must consider these. The relation between belief and the will is very critical for the assessment of faith and cannot reasonably be disregarded by anyone considering the theory of knowledge.

Faith in Its Religious Context

No phenomenon with such striking peculiarities could fail to be controversial. But to understand why faith has these peculiar features, we have to look at the religious traditions that have laid such stress upon it. What follows is not an attempt to argue that the teachings of any one of these traditions are true, only an attempt to see why those who think they are true believe faith to have such importance and value.

These traditions teach that the world is the creation of a God on whom it completely depends but who depends in no way upon it. Although he in no way depends upon it, he is concerned with what happens in it and has acted on that concern by intervening in the world on at least some occasions in human history. These are *theistic* religions. (Theism is distinct from deism, which also holds that the world is the creation of God but denies that he intervenes in it once he has created it, even though he may be well disposed toward it and particularly toward us.⁵)

Theistic religions need not say that God intervenes in the world frequently, however. Certainly in modern scientific times theists are usually anxious to deny any suggestion that their beliefs run counter to the scientific understanding of our world. That understanding requires us to think of the world as one that follows regular and predictable patterns, which scientists discover. The theistic view of the world has to be conformable to the knowledge of it that we have been able to acquire by thinking in this way. This conformity is achieved by viewing those regular sequences as being themselves the outcome of God's will. This vision of the world is found in the first chapter of Genesis: "God said, 'Let there be light'; and there was light." The fact that in this story there was light before there was a sun may indicate that the story is a myth. But the very fact that in the myth God is able to have light without first creating a sun emphasizes the supposed fact about the creation that is the core of the myth's teaching: God does not have to bring about the light by creating the sun first, and if we live in a world where light does come from the sun, that is merely and wholly because he has chosen this sequence.

It is as well for us that natural events have been chosen by God in natural sequences because this enables us to acquire some understanding of them and to exercise some degree of control over them. That we are able to achieve some understanding and control is also something that, on this view of the world, God has chosen should be so and need not have been so. It has an important implication: Every time we use our knowledge of the regularities of the natural world, we freely set in motion some sequence that God has structured. If an archer shoots an arrow, the archer aims and releases it; but it is then carried to its target by processes that the archer no longer controls and that are created by God.⁶ Our freedom, and the power it implies to understand and to control the natural order, inevitably involves us (if theism is true) in a day-to-day cooperation with the will of God. We can see this from the fact that God carries the arrow to wherever the archer aims it, and if the archer has aimed it wrongly, the arrow will be carried to the wrong place. Such things happen all the time. But (on this view of things) they are the consequence of our having a limited degree of freedom and therefore of power. Both are there because God has given them to us.

With freedom and power comes responsibility. Theists think that God has given this to us and that we have misused our freedom and power. We have damaged and corrupted the world into which he has placed us. But they also think that God has given us power and freedom out of love and that he accordingly views our responsibility mercifully rather than vengefully. (This combination of power and mercy is expressed in the image of God as an almighty father that characterizes the Christian tradition.) In consequence, he has not left us without some guidance as to how our power is to be used—all the theistic traditions see our capacity for moral judgment to be due to God's concern for us. He is not hostile or indifferent when we ignore the guidance he has given us and spoil and corrupt the world in which he has placed us.

But if we have been given even a limited degree of power and have misused it, the world we inhabit will have been damaged in a way that confronts our successors with problems that are worse than those that earlier faced us and may well be beyond their capacity to repair, even if they are willing, as we have not been, to follow the guidance available. God's love and mercy will prompt him to intervene. But if he intervenes in a way that is immediately sufficient to repair the damage, he will have taken away from our descendants the autonomy that we have had. So he has to intervene in a way that preserves their autonomy without leaving the damage beyond hope of correction.

The basic requirement of such intervention is the provision of *reassurance* for those who wish to follow the will of God but would otherwise be driven to despair at the apparent hopelessness of their efforts. To be reassured in this way, those who have recognized their own guilt but are conscious of their own powerlessness need some sign that in following God's will, they are in fact acting in a way that will ultimately lead to the creation (or re-creation) of a world that is no longer corrupted because his will will be followed universally. The sign need not consist in the sudden acquisition of miraculous powers, although if it does reassure God's followers, it will by that very fact empower them to a noticeable degree.

The three great theistic religions all teach that in one way or another God has intervened by giving a sign or signs of this kind and that we can take assurance and gain empowerment from this. Each teaches that the signs have come at definite times in history: in the choosing of a people who are given the Law to light the world; in the person of a man having a unique relation to God, whose life and death offer a way of redemption; in the revelation through the Prophet of the way of salvation through submission.[7]

Each tradition, then, claims that God has intervened for us by giving us a *revelation*. The meaning of this notion is highly controversial, but there can be no doubt that it contains a core element of teaching: about God's will, about how we fall short of it, and about what we can do to change. Faith is viewed in all three religions as the positive response to this revelation by the individuals for whom it is intended.

If we place faith in its religious context in this way, some of its puzzling features become intelligible. First, the emphasis on faith's voluntary character can be seen to be essential. For if the purpose of revelation is to reassure us and enable us to live better, it can fail because we do not want to live better badly enough to let ourselves be reassured. We are then guilty of a refusal to acknowledge the needs the revelation addresses and the possibility of self-improvement it offers. We refuse to admit we are in as bad a way as we are told we are and decline to change ourselves in the way the revelation tells us we should. Hence unbelief is identified as a core form of sin. Second, if the revelation that the three religions speak of has come about in history, many, if not most, of those it is aimed at have obviously failed, by choice or circumstance, to recognize it in the required way. In their view, therefore, it is either obviously false or at least not obviously true. If the revelation is true, the signs of its truth have not been convincing to more than a minority.

This leads us to the third, and most initially exasperating, aspect of faith: It is most applauded when the response it embodies is most complete and all embracing. Although intelligible if faith is indeed a response to a revelation from God, this facet of faith in our three religious traditions is exasperating because the wholeheartedness of the response (or the completeness of the reassurance) bears no relation to the quality of the evidence available to the person who manifests it. The applause even seems to get louder when the evidence is weak or when it seems to show up the proclamations as highly improbable. This third feature may be intelligible enough in the light of the story we have told, but it seems to mark out faith as a manifestly irrational state of mind with which the standards definitive of philosophical thought must necessarily be at odds.

The relationship between faith and philosophy in Western thought has never been a comfortable one, and we have now seen why. The result of this discomfort has been a number of philosophical attempts to say what faith is and to address the puzzles to which it gives rise. We must first look at the most important and influential of these.

Notes

1. The term *phenomenological* is used to indicate that the academic study of religions is neutral about their claims to truth. Such matters are said to be "bracketed." For a discussion of religion as an academic pursuit and its neutrality, see Smart 1973. An allied but distinct use of the term, which appears later in this book, is to refer to the way some process is felt or experienced within the consciousness of a subject.

2. In addition to these considerations, it is important for the student to recognize that the major religious traditions have absorbed and generated immense amounts of philosophy and that the relationship cannot be dismissed as a merely external one. For an illustration, see Vesey 1989; and Murti 1960.

3. For further comment on Aquinas and Pascal and their understandings of faith, see Chapter 2.

4. See, for example, what Paul (if it is indeed Paul) says of himself in 2 Timothy 4:7.

5. See Byrne 1989.

6. This is a fact of which the faithful are reminded in the koranic sura "The Spoils," revealed after the Battle of Badr (624).

7. I ignore at this point the judgments of the traditions on each other.

CHAPTER TWO

Faith and Western Philosophy

We have seen why the relationship between faith and philosophy has always been an uneasy one in the Western world. In this chapter I propose to outline some of the major attempts philosophers have made to reach an estimate of faith and its rationality (or lack of it).

Before Aquinas

Western philosophical thought did not begin in response to religious claims. It is commonly believed that philosophy's early development among the Greeks was due to deliberate and self-conscious emancipation from the mythical thought forms in which Greek religious life was expressed.[1] However this may be, there is no doubt that philosophy as we have come to know it reached full maturity in the hands of Socrates, Plato, and Aristotle without its major practitioners feeling the need to integrate it with the religious life of their communities. This is unaffected by such well-known facts as the importance of Socrates' inner voice, the enormous attraction of Platonic categories throughout the history of Christian theology, and the religious instructions in Aristotle's will.[2] The main reason that even the systems that later gave such nourishment to Western religious thinkers were not integrated with religion by their originators is that Greek religion was polytheistic, not monotheistic. The gods were beings whose reality may have gone unquestioned and whose power frequently intruded itself into human life and had to be propitiated. In many ways the Greeks were a highly religious people. But it did not occur to the major thinkers of classical times to identify fundamental cosmic principles with personal deities. To Greek thinkers the gods were themselves beings within the cosmos and therefore subject, as we are, to whatever principles govern it. They did not envisage the possibility that such principles could themselves be personal in nature. But when their successors had to undertake the task of integrating philosophical thought with the Judeo-Christian tradition, this became the first doctrinal requirement their thinking had to satisfy.[3]

When Christianity appeared on the scene, it did not appear as one more religion but as an implacable rival to all others. It claimed total allegiance from everyone. (Judaism, of course, had denied the claims of all other gods but did not proselytize.) When thinkers of philosophical bent accepted Christianity, they had to contend with the fact that philosophical speculations seemed unnecessary and religiously hazardous to many of their fellow Christians. But the resources of Greek philosophical thought were nevertheless rapidly drawn upon to respond to the hostile criticisms of pagan thinkers and to articulate what Christian commitments were—in particular, to distinguish orthodox from heretical teachings. Once this happened, it became obvious that some philosophical traditions were full of valuable and recognizable theological resources; their usefulness seemed to be a provision of divine providence. So in spite of the existence, from early years, of a vigorous tradition of fideism (the view that faith does not need the support of reason and should not seek it), represented most famously in ancient times by Tertullian, philosophical concepts and arguments found their way into the theology, apologetics, and even doctrinal statements of the Christian tradition.[4]

Many of the key themes of Western philosophical reflection on faith make their first appearance in the works of Augustine, even though it would be an error to suppose that he offers a full theory of what faith is. The most fundamental feature of Augustine's thought on this matter is that faith is a condition of understanding. This teaching has two main aspects. First, he believes the ultimate vision of truth that Plato saw as the goal of the philosopher is in fact the vision of God that comes to the faithful hereafter, in eternity. This vision is not available to us without divine grace, as pagan philosophers had supposed. Second, he believes that the lesser sorts of knowledge that are available to us in this life also require a prior form of faith and acceptance of authority. Augustine, the author of the first systematic critique of philosophical skepticism, holds that both in ordinary life and in matters of salvation suspense of judgment is an impossible goal. To these themes, which both became common features of later apologetic writing, we must add the best-known Augustinian doctrine of the corruption of the human will. Faith is an antidote to this corruption and enables us to grow toward the love of God that will find its goal in the beatific vision; but since corruption of the human will by sin is a barrier even to the acceptance of the church's proclamations, so faith itself is a product of the grace of God. This latter teaching combines two themes that reappear in Aquinas: the doctrine that belief depends not only upon the intellect but also upon the will (that believing is something that we choose to do or not to do) and the doctrine that without the intervention of God, the choice to believe the key truths of faith would not be made.[5]

The most important medieval thinker to follow closely in Augustine's footsteps is Saint Anselm. He is best known to philosophers for his famous Ontological Argument for the existence of God, to be found in the *Proslogion*. This is famous as an apparent attempt to prove the reality of God through an analysis, or definition, of the concept of God itself. Thus described, it is as extreme an example as one could imagine of an attempt to replace faith by reasoning. But it is clear that Anselm does not see his purpose in this way. In the first place, the *Proslogion* is in the form of a prayer or address to God, whose being is therefore clearly presupposed before the probative exercise begins. In the second place, Anselm clearly states a principle that Augustine had pronounced: "I do not seek to understand that I may believe, but I believe in order to understand. For this I also believe—that unless I believed, I should not understand."[6] Anselm clearly sees faith as a precondition of whatever sort of cognitive satisfaction reason is able to gain in its service.

But it is difficult to square this with the elaboration of arguments. Faith may well provide a necessary motive for certain kinds of philosophical activity, such as the attempt to persuade unbelievers. But if the argument generated in this way is sound, it will be sound because it satisfies standards that are independent of faith.

An argument that can be seen to be sound only by someone who already accepts its conclusion is likely to be a defective one.

Aquinas

The most systematic and influential account of faith and its relation to reason is the one we find in Saint Thomas Aquinas. Here, as elsewhere, Thomas's debt to Augustine is a considerable one. Thomas accepts that the will plays an essential role in the formation of belief as well as the intellect and that faith, when we find it, is therefore due to the infusion of the grace of God since the human will is not capable of leading us to it without such aid. But Thomas views the role of natural human reason more positively.

The philosophical tradition with which Aquinas integrates his theological thought is that of Aristotle rather than that of Plato—a fact deriving from the recovery of Aristotle's thought in the West during the High Middle Ages. This recovery was due to the fact that Aristotle's major writings had been preserved by Muslim scholars. One of the two great theological works for which Aquinas is famous, the *Summa Contra Gentiles,* was reputedly compiled as a manual of argument to be used against the Muslims, whose scholars shared not only a common belief in one God but also the knowledge of this philosophical tradition.

Like Augustine, Aquinas holds that the ultimate good for human nature is the enjoyment of the vision of God. But this vision is not possible for us in this mortal life since our minds must always begin from information supplied us by the senses. Human reason can move beyond sensory information in science and philosophy and can arrive at vitally important truths through abstraction and argument. It can even show us that there is a God and that he directs the course of the world and of history. This activity of the natural reason came later to be known as natural theology.

Natural theology is a form of knowledge (*scientia*) that does not require grace to be successfully pursued. It does not enable us to penetrate the nature of the supernatural reality it shows us to exist, however. Nor is it either necessary or sufficient for salvation. This is just as well; for if it were necessary, only the learned could attain to salvation, and most people would have neither the time nor the ability to attain it. Fortunately there is another way in which God has enabled us to be directed in this life toward the vision of him that he wishes us to share. This is the way of revelation, and faith is the response to revelation that God's grace enables us to make.[7]

The fundamental principle of Thomas's thought is that grace does not destroy nature but perfects it. Hence natural reason should serve faith as the natural inclination of the will serves charity (or the love of God).[8] Just as our natural inclination to seek what is good leads us by nature toward God but needs to be augmented by the gift of divine grace before we can love him, so our ability to prove the reality of God and his providence must be completed by grace for us to assent to those truths about himself and our relationship to him that he has revealed for the sake of our salvation. These truths are to be found in the scriptures and in the doctrinal pronouncements of the church, especially the creeds. By the time of Aquinas the church was not a struggling body of mostly poor adherents living in a pagan world where its claims were politically suspect but had long been the leading cultural and spiritual institution in a civilization that prided itself on being Christian. So the faith that the church required of its members was a matter of accepting the truths that its scriptures contained and that it had the authority to interpret.

The assent of the faithful to the truths thus revealed, though requiring the grace of God, represents a perfecting of what reason can show (and for some has shown) to us in two ways. First, someone for whom natural reason has shown there is a God who governs the world might well expect there to be available a revelation of his plan of human salvation just as the church says there is. Second, the claims that the church makes are not just dogmatic assertions that do not commend themselves to the intellect; the scriptures contain many prophecies that history shows to have been fulfilled, and there have been many miracles that attest to the authority of those who have proclaimed the church's message. These "preambles to faith," as they are known, show that the church has rational credentials and that the assent to its proclamations that the faithful express when they recite the creed is at least similar to the assent that they give in matters where natural reason is sovereign. So although faith is not a product of natural reason, it is nevertheless a rational state.

Yet it is not rational in the same manner as natural knowledge is because the truths to which we assent in faith are mysteries: The nature of God is beyond our intellect's power to understand. For example, even though our intellect can show us unaided that God ex-

ists, it cannot tell us his nature. More important still for our present
purposes, many of the truths we assent to in faith that are essential
for our salvation are not merely mysteries whose nature is beyond
us but are such that we could not without revelation know them
even to be so. Without revelation, for example, we could not be
aware that the one God is a unity of three persons or that Jesus is
the son of God.

Faith is rational in three ways. Some of its truths (such as the being of God), though also revealed, can be proved by natural reason.
Others that cannot be so proved are still attested by evidences. And
we can infer that whenever some revealed doctrine, such as the
Incarnation, appears to be contrary to reason, this is indeed only
apparent, and the arguments of heretics or infidels against it can be
shown to be sophistries.

Although these three conditions are true, Aquinas merely sees
this as showing that faith is rational and not foolish, not that the
philosopher is needed to legitimize faith or, in language much used
today, to provide it with foundations. This latter is a modern notion
that I discuss later, but it is misleading to assume that because
Aquinas makes the rationality of faith central to the apologetic enterprise, he sees philosophy as providing faith with authority.

Aquinas also gives us a detailed analysis of the nature of faith itself. It is the first of the three supernatural (or theological) virtues,
the others being hope and charity (or love). These virtues are supernatural because we cannot attain them ourselves; they require an infusion of grace. In the case of faith, grace enables the will to move
the intellect to assent to the truths of revelation and to do so wholeheartedly and assuredly. Virtues, whether natural or supernatural,
are habits (or dispositions) to act in certain ways; the acts that manifest the virtue of faith are the inner act of belief and the outer, or
public, act of confession. Belief (*credere*) in the articles of faith differs in a key respect from the sort of assent we give to secular matters when we have to weigh evidence and form an opinion (*opinio*).
In this latter case, our assent is given "with fear of the opposite."
But the assent given in the case of faith is "firmly attached to one alternative," and in this respect the state of mind of the faithful believer is like that of the person who has knowledge (*scientia*).

In other language, the believer has a degree of certainty or assurance that is like that of the person who has reached the conclusion
of a demonstration. But since faith is a virtue, the assent it involves

must have merit, and it would not have any if it were arrived at be-cause of conclusive reasons; for then one could not *withhold* the as-sent one gives. To say yes to something that has been proved is not meritorious because one cannot say no. The certainty that faith in-volves is meritorious, so it must be freely given. This is the result of the divine empowerment of the will, which directs the intellect to say yes. It is not the result of proof. It follows from this that the ev-idences (such as miracles and fulfilled prophecies) that make the as-sent of faith to revelation a rational assent cannot, in spite of this, be conclusive, or the merit of faith would be taken away. It also fol-lows that those philosophers who manage to prove some of the truths that revelation contains (such as the existence of God) do not hold to *those* propositions as a part of their faith, though the larger majority of persons, who only learn of them through revelation, do. Faith and knowledge, then, are exclusive. Faith involves volun-tary assent to the truths of revelation, to which the will is disposed by a special infusion of grace. This enables the believer to assent with steadfastness and certainty, which the absence of conclusive grounds would otherwise make impossible.[9]

This typically subtle and ingenious account of faith raises impor-tant questions. There is a tension between Thomas's insistence on the rationality of faith and his insistence on its voluntary character, a tension that has been reflected in subsequent Catholic teaching about the status of the evidences for faith.[10] The resolution of this tension depends on the claim that there is a necessary connection between the voluntariness of faith and the fact that its propositions are not proved to us—that is, a necessary exclusion of faith and knowledge. Yet this exclusion does not extend to the admission of uncertainty or doubt into faith—an uncertainty or a doubt that can well obtain in the case of secular belief (or opinion). So the analysis of faith that emerges makes its certainty meritorious for the very reason that it holds in the face of evidence that is less than conclu-sive. This makes the differences between the views of Aquinas and the views of later thinkers such as Kierkegaard much less than they are commonly thought to be.

It would be seriously misleading not to include here a mention of Thomas's distinction between formed and unformed faith. This distinction is intended to recognize the place of growth in faith in the religious life. Faith as the first of the three theological virtues is completed, or formed, by the addition of hope and love. The love of God that characterizes such a life is a love that enriches the assent that the believer gives to the truths of the faith. When the believer first assents to those truths, he or she cannot yet do so out of a love for God and so will not yet have a formed or completed faith; the believer will merely be on the road to it. The first assent will still, however, be a gift from God.[11] The grace of God is at work whenever anyone acquires faith—hence the certainty that it embodies, even when the will is not fully turned to God in charity.

But Thomas now has a special problem in the case of the devils who are said by Saint James to believe and to tremble.[12] They are forced by signs to believe in the same truths that those who have faith believe, but they are not motivated by the will toward the good that motivates even those who have unformed faith. He seems to say (though he departs from his usual high level of clarity here) that the devils have faith, but of some inferior, unmeritorious third kind, as a result of assenting to the signs of God's power and the "acumen of their natural intelligence."[13] The problem here is not one that goes away if we disregard the mythology of the demons, for Thomas's attempt to incorporate the awkward scriptural passage here forces him to acknowledge that it is possible for someone to be convinced by signs of the truth that he or she at least thinks are conclusive but accepts reluctantly. It is not clear whether Aquinas thinks this takes away from the voluntariness of the assent or merely from its merit.[14] Whatever the answer, the connection among merit, rationality, and voluntariness seems less tidy than Thomas's account of faith initially suggests it is.

After Aquinas

The Catholic synthesis of Greek philosophical thought and Christian theology that reached its most powerful expression in Thomism was attacked and undermined by both the theological changes of the Protestant Reformation and the development of modern philosophy. For our present purposes it is only possible at this stage to include mention of the different (or apparently different) understanding of faith that we find in the teachings of Martin Luther. The understanding of faith that Thomas offers us clearly makes it the first, but only the first, of the theological virtues and stresses that its essence is the acceptance and proclamation of the truths proclaimed by the church. The main thrust of the Reformers was the rejection of the claims of the Catholic church to be the authoritative interpreter of revelation, which was said instead to be confined to the scriptures, and the insistence that salvation is a matter, not of submission to ecclesiastical authority and especially not of the performance of sanctifying works, but of individual trust in God. Faith, as Luther interpets it, is sufficient, not merely necessary, for salvation and is a matter of trusting God's promises rather than acceding to propositions.

It is easy to exaggerate the differences between this view of faith and the one we find in Thomas. Thomas, for example, maintains that the faithful accept the church's proclamations because they judge them to come from God.[15] But there is no doubt that the change in emphasis is an important one that in the long run entails a different understanding of what revelation is as well as a different understanding of the faithful's response to it. For the present I merely note that the concept of trust itself cries out for philosophical analysis; I try to provide some comments on it later in this work.[16]

Faith, Skepticism, and Foundationalism

Recent defenses of religious faith have often emphasized the extent to which philosophical criticism of it has depended on what are called foundationalist assumptions. These are more often mentioned and deplored than they are defined. Roughly, foundationalism is a manifestation of the fact that many philosophers have tended to think it their special function to decide on the rationality of the activities and judgments of others, including, of course, themselves when they are playing other roles. Hence there exists the philosophy *of* this and that, such as science, morals, or aesthetic judgment—at least when these activities appear to set standards rather than merely report on them. (When they merely report on them and seek only to tell us what standards others follow independently of philosophy, they are sometimes described as naturalistic inquiries.)

Foundationalist attitudes to the role of philosophy go back at least as far as Socrates, who was put to death for insisting that the philosopher should require others to examine, and if necessary replace, the standards on which their choices depend and who clearly believed that the philosopher can develop an expertise that gives his enterprise priority over others'. But foundationalism in modern times has had a central epistemological preoccupation, which is due primarily to Descartes and to a lesser extent to Locke.

Descartes, who is commonly said to have been the founder of modern philosophy, tells us that he is "beginning again from the very foundations." This he must do "if I would secure some sure and lasting result in science."[17] The objective is the secular one of underpinning *science.* But the connection of this objective with religious faith is never so very far from Descartes's mind and is a constant preoccupation of philosophers in the early modern period.

Few things are better known about Descartes than the fact that he begins his search for the foundations of knowledge by developing a form of extreme skeptical doubt and that he then tries to establish knowledge on a firm footing by answering that doubt step by step. It is still less well understood than it should be that in following this procedure, Descartes is not slaying an imaginary foe but is responding to an influential revival of the Skeptic thought of antiquity.[18] This revival had considerable theological implications.

Greek Skepticism is traced to Pyrrho (ca. 365–ca. 270 B.C.) and receives its fullest documentary expression in Cicero and Sextus Empiricus, the latter in the third century A.D.[19] Roughly, the Skeptics followed Socrates in questioning all received opinions but did not share his optimism that these could be replaced by anything more assured. Indeed, the essence of their stance was their unwillingness to "dogmatize" or form theories. The Skeptics were rivals of the Epicureans and Stoics of the Hellenistic era and, like them, sought inner calm or serenity. The Skeptic, however, did not claim to find this through the discovery of the truth about our place in the cosmos and the nature of the good. The Skeptic failed to find any satisfaction in the many theories that others developed on these themes and after an exhaustive examination of their inadequacies reached a stage of suspended judgment (*epoche*). Inner calm, known to the Skeptic as *ataraxia,* or unperturbedness, was said to follow such suspense. To the accusation that suspense of judgment on everything was impossible, the Skeptic replied that suspense was followed by an undogmatic return to the appearances, that is, to the common opinions, sensory and practical, that dogmatists had sought without success to ground in theoretical certainties. The Skeptic, in other words, abandoned the Socratic search for knowledge and reverted to a conformity with the practices and opinions of his time and place without supposing that these were any more than expressions of how things seemed to those in his historical and social situation. It was not that he judged the truth to be unattainable (which would in its turn have been a form of negative dogmatism), but that he accepted that he had so far not found it and would live in accordance with how things seemed to him, free of what we would today call ideology.

The new beginning that Descartes tried to give to philosophy was the result of his wish to provide a definitive refutation of the Pyrrhonist tradition. Pyrrhonism had enjoyed a revival through the rediscovery of the writings of Sextus Empiricus in the sixteenth century. One of the sources of interest was the fact that it provided ammunition for one side in the debate between Catholics and Protestants, a debate that on the surface was precisely the kind of ideological battle the Skeptic would have evaded.

Classical Skepticism had not been antireligious. The Pyrrhonist had conformed to the religious forms current in his own society and had done so undogmatically (or without belief). To those at the time of Descartes who were faced with the bitter disputes between Catholicism and Protestantism, the obvious difficulty of the Protestant case was its insistence that each individual believer had to reach his or her own inner illumination and understanding of scripture. To the Catholic mind this was a sure recipe for faction and chaos. One source of escape from such chaos was the stance of the Catholic Pyrrhonist, who saw the institutionalized practices and interpretations of the church as the established religious forms to which the bewildered inquirer could gratefully conform. Hence there emerged a conformist kind of fideism, worlds apart from the synthesis of faith and reason found in Aquinas, that seemed to offer religious peace at the price of abandoning all serious claims to knowledge, religious or secular. The most famous and seductive expression (or apparent expression) of this stance was found in Montaigne, against whom both Descartes and Pascal, in their very different ways, were reacting.[20]

For all his orthodoxy, Descartes's primary concern is not the defense of a more traditional faith but the establishment of scientific knowledge. The Pyrrhonist questioned all attempts to attain a form of knowledge that transcends appearances. To refute Pyrrhonian skepticism, Descartes carries some of its arguments considerably further than its classical representatives had carried them. In doing this, he consciously leaves behind the practical and moral motivations of the Greek Skeptics and engages in purely theoretical exercises that he says no one would seriously engage in in practice—doubting the reliability of the senses and the claims of theoretical reason. His purpose is to find truths of which no doubt whatsoever is possible. He first finds that he cannot, however he might try, doubt the fact of his own existence. From this he infers that he is a thinking (or conscious) being (*res cogitans*). It emerges from these two foundational truths that even if his thoughts and perceptions do not match any outer reality, he cannot be in error about what his thoughts and perceptions are.

These results dictate a new epistemological program for modern philosophy. Where the Pyrrhonian skeptic contented himself with appearances and suspended judgment about whatever reality lay behind them, such a skeptic is replaced in post-Cartesian thought by another sort of doubter. The post-Cartesian doubter accepts that he or she has knowledge of his or her own inner states but needs to be assured that there even is a physical universe beyond them. This doubter even needs assurance that there are other conscious subjects. The Pyrrhonian never questioned this but assumed it to be so since Pyrrhonian doubt was about whether the conventional opinions of the community of perceivers correctly represented reality. The Cartesian skeptic faces what is sometimes called the egocentric predicament, in which one knows oneself and one's inner states and replaces doubt about the external world by extending this minimal knowledge outward.

It is here that we find the "foundationalism" of modern philosophy at its source. The attempt to refute skepticism begins with starting points that even the most resolute skeptic cannot deny and assesses other knowledge claims by determining whether they can be inferred from these starting points. The starting points are thought to be indubitable because they are within the subject's own consciousness and are therefore uniquely accessible to an inquirer.

Descartes's attempt to move from these inner starting points to knowledge of the world depends, notoriously, on his attempt to demonstrate the veracity of clear and distinct ideas; this demonstration requires him to argue that one of the ideas in his consciousness, that of God, could not be there if there were no being without to correspond to it.[21] This proof of God supposedly guarantees the analysis of clear and distinct concepts as the method of scientific advance. But later thinkers who did not seek to follow him in this "circular" argument still assumed a foundationalist program, though they may have sought to ground the advance of knowledge on different starting points, such as the awareness of sensory impressions.

Descartes's purpose was to show that properly founded scientific claims could be accepted as truths about an outer reality, not as mere ways of accommodating the mind to appearances. But skepticism was not the only enemy here. The skeptics had never prevented actual scientific advances; they had merely caused their philosophical colleagues to hesitate about the significance of these advances. The church, however, *had* interfered with scientific advance—most famously by its condemnation of Galileo.[22] Cartesianism provided a theoretical basis for the assumption, now deeply embedded in our culture, that such interference represented an improper confusion between the distinct roles of theology and natural science. Natural science was indeed a source of truth about the physical world; but the purposes that God might have in its creation and the spiritual purposes that move us outside scientific inquiry were not within the domain of natural science. The famous Cartesian dualism of the mental and the physical was a metaphysical expression of the complete separateness of the spheres of theology and science. Where Aquinas had viewed secular learning and theological truth as continuous and mutually reinforcing, Descartes ensures their separation. This separation has, in combination with epistemological foundationalism, led to a deep shift in the philosophical assumptions about faith and reason—a shift that some influential contemporary philosophers of religion are trying to reverse.

Descartes had himself admitted, indeed stressed, that the skeptical doubts about the foundations of scientific knowledge that he explored and tried to answer were of purely theoretical interest; that in practice no one, and certainly no practicing scientific inquirer, would find them a hindrance to investigation. So the foundationalist attempts to ground scientific knowledge by inferring its contents from some privileged class of basic truths was always supposed to end with the endorsement of actual scientific achievements. But the very separation of such achievements from most forms of religious thinking suggests that a foundationalist epistemological program would also put religious beliefs into question. The philosopher, or at least the epistemologist, increasingly came to be seen as someone who adjudicates the claims of revelation by seeing whether the human mind can establish (from its approved starting points) the reality of the God to whose supposed revelation faith is a response. The prior success of natural theology comes in modern times to be regarded as a necessary condition of the rationality of faith.

The Post-Cartesian Challenge to Faith

The erosion of the Thomistic synthesis of secular and religious knowledge took some time to become apparent. There were two phases in this process. The first consisted of the separation of the two intellectual supports of faith in the Thomistic system, namely, the arguments of natural theology and the evidences for revelation. The second consisted of challenges to the very possibility of the former.

The philosophical literature of the seventeenth century is filled with the arguments of natural theology. Descartes himself uses the Ontological Argument, as do Leibniz and Spinoza. The Cosmological Proof is used by Descartes and Leibniz and later receives its most telling modern formulation at the hands of Samuel Clarke.[23] But it was the Argument from Design that became more and more popular. Aquinas had rejected the Ontological Argument; and the versions of the Cosmological Argument that we find in the first three of his Five Ways are not radically different from the form the argument later takes in Clarke. But the Design Argument came to be very different in form from the version Aquinas had used in his Fifth Way. The latter derived from the Aristotelian natural philosophy and argued that the teleological structure of natural phenomena requires explanation by reference to God.[24] Since the growth of modern physical science came about largely through the abandonment of Aristotelian teleology, the Design Argument now assumed a different form in which the divine mind was inferred as the architect of the cosmic machinery described in Newtonian physics. The most famous version of the argument was the one presented, late in the debate, by Paley, but its proponents were very numerous and included Newton himself.[25] The argument was widely used and widely thought to be virtually irrefutable, perhaps because, unlike the Ontological and Cosmological Proofs, it seemed itself to be based on reasoning from evidence in the way natural science was thought to be.

But the mechanical planner of the Design Argument was not obviously the God of Abraham, Isaac, and Jacob, who intervenes in history and reveals himself in miracle and prophecy. Indeed, some began to say that if God had occasion to act in this way, he would not seem to have planned the cosmos as neatly as Newton had shown him to have done. Instead of its seeming obvious now that a proof of God's existence would make the truth of the historical claims of Christianity more likely, the demonstration of the Designing God seemed to many to turn its signs and wonders into otiose fables. This was the position of the deists, who proposed that we confine ourselves to natural (or humanly demonstrable) religion and disregard the revealed religion the churches sought to base upon it.

The person most responsible for this development in English thought, though unintentionally, was John Locke, now regarded, with Descartes, as cofounder of modern epistemological foundationalism. In his *Essay Concerning Human Understanding* he seeks to trace all knowledge to sources in sensory experience and our responses to it. At the very end of the *Essay,* and in his last work, *The Reasonableness of Christianity,* he seeks to show that the new epistemology does not undermine religious faith, even though faith may require us to accept doctrines that are "above reason." The latter are not *contrary* to reason, that is, not logically absurd. But they may be "against the probable conjectures of reason," that is, improbable. We may still be justified in accepting such doctrines if they are revealed to us. But when? He insists that whether a supposed revelation is true is a matter that God has given us our reason to determine. Our reason can determine favorably and not leave faith at the mercy of mere religious illumination, or "enthusiasm," if those who proclaim the revelations can show us that God has accompanied them with "outward signs." These are the miracles and the fulfilled prophecies of the Christian tradition—that is, the traditional evidences of the faith.[26]

Revelation therefore has to have rationally acceptable credentials. If it does, we are entitled to accept doctrines that are in themselves beyond anything that reason could suggest to us. What Locke's deistic successors did was to insist that if reason is indeed the authority that determines whether a supposed revelation is acceptable, it should rule out all doctrines that reason itself cannot vouch for. In saying this, they were merely drawing different results from a line of reasoning that Locke had taught them. They tended to do this in a nominally Christian context, as we can see from the titles of the two most famous deistic treatises: John Toland's *Christianity Not Mysterious* (1696) and Matthew Tindal's *Christianity as Old as the Creation* (1730). Each sought to argue that revealed religion is an ignorant person's version of a natural religion that can dispense with its stories, wonders, and pieties.

The deists did not have everything their own way. Joseph Butler's *The Analogy of Religion* (1736) is a sustained and effective argument that if one accepts that our world is designed by God, one should not be so confident as the deists were that he would not have additional purposes that he might show in special revelation. It is therefore imprudent to close off this possibility a priori and not examine the claims of Christian revelation with care. But this argument left open the possibility that the basic premise the deists shared with their orthodox opponents—namely, the obviousness of God's design in nature—could itself be put in question.

It was put in question by Hume and Kant. It is not possible here to explore their criticisms of natural theology, which have been largely accepted into the received wisdom of contemporary philosophy.[27] Hume shows the radical defects of the Design Argument in the *Dialogues Concerning Natural Religion* (1779), in which its pretension to be a well-founded scientific inference is shown to be baseless. In the still-neglected *Natural History of Religion* (1757), he pioneers in the anthropology of religion, arguing that actual religious practice is not founded on a philosophical perception of cosmic order but is a response to the fears generated by unpredicted natural disasters. When these works are considered alongside his most famous antireligious essay, the section "Of Miracles" in his *Enquiry Concerning Human Understanding,* we have a threefold onslaught on religious orthodoxy that presents it as having no intellectual foundation, leaning on weak historical evidences, and being a product of "sick men's dreams." In the dialectic of the *Critique of Pure Reason* (1781), Kant produces classic refutations of all the major forms of proof of God's existence, claiming that they are all illegitimate extensions of reason beyond the sphere of possible experience.

This erosion of the intellectual foundations of faith, as these had been perceived in the early modern period, left a widespread perception that faith is groundless and irrational. In our own day this perception is being questioned by those religious thinkers who maintain that its rationality does not depend on the existence of the intellectual foundations that the Enlightenment thinkers demanded. We consider some of their arguments at a later stage. First, however, we must conclude our sampling of the intellectual history of the debates on faith and reason by examining the fideistic tradition, with which these contemporary arguments have some affinities.

Skeptical Fideism

Just as the assertion of a foundational role for philosophy has ancient roots, so does its religious rejection. In the modern era, however, the Cartesian conjunction of foundationalism with the refutation of skepticism has also had a fideistic counterpart. In this the skeptic has been seen as someone who exposes the pretensions of reason and therefore may make faith easier, regardless of whether it is his intention to do so. From such a standpoint the attacks on natural theology made by Hume and Kant can appear as blessings in disguise since they head off all attempts to support faith through argument.[28]

We can find what I call the conformist version of skeptical fideism in the work of Montaigne and Bayle, who seem to evade the stresses of religious faction by imitating the undogmatic observance characteristic of the Greek Skeptics. But the two fideistic thinkers who have exercised the greatest influence have been Pascal and Kierkegaard. In neither case is a serious summary possible; I instead merely indicate certain dominant themes of importance in later parts of this work.

At the time of his death in 1662, Pascal left unfinished an Apology for the Christian Religion that is now known as the *Pensées*. As it stands, it is still the greatest work of Christian apologetics that there is or is likely to be. Pascal seeks to lead his reader toward conversion through self-knowledge. Human beings are solitary and anxious. Their plight reveals a paradoxical combination of potential greatness and squalor. They seek to escape this plight through reason. Even though human reason is a unique sign of humanity's higher destiny, the attempts of philosophers to rescue us from the evils of the human condition are doomed to failure. In spite of Descartes's attempts to prove otherwise, reason is powerless to supply the basis on which common sense and science depend. Fortunately our natures supply the antidote to skepticism that reason cannot supply: The first principles on which human thought depends are supplied by the heart, not the reason. But although the skeptic is unable to make us doubt the truths on which daily life depends, he is nevertheless right to expose the incapacity of reason to lead us to God. Attempts to reach God through reason can lead only to a facile form of deism, not a real faith. For this we need to attend to the signs of God's presence that are all around us but that the corruption of the heart prevents us from recognizing. Faith is God known by the heart, or innermost personality, not the reason. Our reason needs to be humbled: The skeptic, in spite of his own foolish arrogance, can assist us in humbling it. Once this is recognized, we can read the signs of God in nature and in the scriptures and can be opened to the workings of God's grace, which Pascal, like Augustine and Aquinas before him, thought necessary before faith can take hold.

Scattered through the *Pensées,* therefore, we find three claims. First, skepticism is unlivable and is prevented by the resources of human nature. Second, reason alone can lead us only to deism, not to real faith. Third, faith comes from an acceptance of the signs of God's revelation in nature and the scriptures, signs that are ambiguous to us until we are ready to open ourselves to them. The last is combined with an argument that has attracted more attention from philosophers than all the rest of Pascal: the famous "Wager" argument. Its precise place in the strategy of the projected apology is not quite clear, as it is not among the fragments that Pascal himself ordered and classified.[29] But it is an argument directed toward someone whose complacency has been shaken by self-examination but who recognizes, through skeptical questioning, that reason cannot tell us whether God exists. Such a person can still be reached by a special sort of prudential reasoning. If God exists, and I have not lived my life as though he does, I shall face the prospect of eternal suffering. If, however, I have lived my life as though God does exist, and he does not, I shall merely, by the time of my death, have lost a few temporal pleasures. With so much at stake, the game of life is clearly one it is in my interest to play by wagering that God does indeed exist.

But such a wager at first glance looks impossible to make. For it seems to require me to believe in something that I do not by hypothesis have any more reason to believe than to disbelieve, namely, the existence of God. But this situation is one that I can correct. I can start to live as though God does exist by attending masses and following other religious observances; I can do this in the hope that I shall *come* to believe in that which it is clearly in my interest to believe rather than not to believe.

Pascal gives us here the classic statement of what we can call prudential theism: the argument that even if there is no better reason to think there is a God than that there is not, we should try to induce belief in ourselves by acting as though we already have it. Pascal's argument has had few admirers, although it has been revived, in a less clear but to some more palatable form, by William James. We have occasion to examine prudential theism later. For the moment it is enough to note two things: First, Pascal does not identify the adoption of the policy he recommends in the Wager fragment with faith itself since faith is the hoped-for outcome of it; second, Pascal does not think belief is something one can command but rather something one can set out to induce.

The last thinker whom there is need to describe briefly is Kierkegaard. Here the barriers to crisp summary are insurmountable, and I once again attempt only to isolate some major themes that we explore more deeply later. (I have to disregard such fundamental exegetical matters as the significance of the pseudonyms, for example.)

Kierkegaard's constant theme is the nature of Christian faith, particularly its unintelligibility to philosophical reason. This does not mean, as many defeated readers have too hastily concluded, that Kierkegaard is not offering us any philosophical theses. He is, as Pascal was. His philosophical thesis is that faith cannot make the sort of sense that philosophical inquiry demands. Faith can only be misrepresented if we seek to make sense of it as an answer to the philosophical quest for understanding or for the good. Like Pascal, Kierkegaard thinks that the skeptic can at least deflect us from supposing that answers to the philosophical quest can be gained through reason; but he goes further and insists that faith does not merely carry us beyond the sphere of reason but is actively offensive or contrary to it. His most famous short work, *Fear and Trembling,* is a series of panegyrics on Abraham, who sets out at the command of God to sacrifice his son, Isaac, even though such a command would seem to negate all the promises God made to Abraham at the time of his original calling. Abraham's mind-set, with its positivity and cheerfulness, does not make the kind of sense that the tragic renunciations of classical heroes make; nor does it make sense by the standards of secular ethics. It is finally justified, but the justification is not something that Abraham is in any position to foresee when he sets out to do what God demands from him. In *Philosophical Fragments* and *Concluding Unscientific Postscript*, Kierkegaard develops another contrast: that between the claims of the philosophical teacher, typified in history by Socrates, and the demands of the divine teacher, namely, Christ. In this contrast Kierkegaard addresses a number of the very deepest questions about faith's nature, most particularly the sort of response or commitment it involves and the historical nature of the revelation to which that commitment is the only answer.

The philosophical teacher seeks to draw out the recognition of truth from the inquirer. But as Socrates shows us in Plato's *Meno*, that approach implies that the inquirer already has the truth within and that the teacher serves merely as a stimulus to its emergence. The teacher can help remove obstructions (that is, confusions and distractions), but the key to the inquirer's enlightenment is within the learner. The teacher, then, is not necessary, and the timing of the encounter between them is historically accidental. On this view, famously, knowledge is not imparted but recalled, and the teacher enters only to stand aside. Those who have been taught by such teachers are grateful to them for releasing powers in themselves they did not fully realize they had. This is the sort of gratitude that exists between equals who vary, at most, in degrees of ability.

It was an attitude like this, which assumes equality, that seems to have been expressed by Nicodemus at the outset of the famous passage in the third chapter of John's gospel—a passage that Kierkegaard does not directly discuss in the *Philosophical Fragments* but that clearly forms part of the inspiration for what he says there. Nicodemus, a Pharisee and leader of the Jews, comes to Jesus by night (that is, away from the crowds) and says that he recognizes that God must be with Jesus because of all the marvelous things he has been doing. On the surface this is a conciliatory, even deferential, gesture, but one that assumes equality. Jesus' response bewilders Nicodemus, who is told, with no reported conversational transition, that he must be born again to see the kingdom of God. What the divine teacher does is to demand a total personal transformation, not the mere realization of a truth. Such a demand, and the response to it, is not something incidental to the hearer's own self-development but something momentous and the decisive historical occasion for the hearer.

It has always been held that Christianity is a uniquely historical religion, making claims about someone who lived at a definite time in history. But Kierkegaard insists that this historicity needs to be understood in a way that does not give special privilege or priority to those who were present at the time when Jesus walked the earth. For many have responded since that time in the right way to the claims that he makes, and many in his own day responded to those claims in the wrong way. Kierkegaard's argument raises the deepest questions about how one is to understand the idea of revelation. The sort of decision that Kierkegaard thinks revelation demands from us is a decision we can refuse to make if we wish. Hence the divine teacher cannot be self-evidently divine. If he were, we would be overwhelmed or would respond out of fear or selfish calculation. We have to be free to miss the point as Nicodemus does. But this implies that the divine teacher (that is, God himself) has to appear in a lowly guise, as a servant, incognito. This is the sort of appearance that can be recognized for what it is or rejected at any time, contemporaneous or later.

This rendering of the doctrine of Incarnation makes the alleged fact of it, and the recognition of it, paradoxical and tries at the same time to show why it has to be. Reason cannot show the divine teacher to be what he is, for if it could, the demand of free submission would be impossible to meet. We find here a reemergence of the view we found in Thomas; that what is proved to us cannot be freely accepted. We also find an ingenious attempt to show the irrelevance of historical difficulties about the textual basis of knowledge of revelation. I conclude with a brief description of the nature of the faith that constitutes the believer's acceptance of that revelation, on Kierkegaard's view.

Reason cannot generate this acceptance. Nor can reason make sense of it. Its attempts to make sense of it merely represent impertinent attempts to domesticate the divine demand and evade it—to prove the certainty or probability of a being one has decided to attempt to ignore. Part of the explanation of this fact is that the object of the response of faith is not a truth in the sense of some proposition but the Person who demands it, that is, God. But Kierkegaard does not cease to talk of faith as entailing the acceptance of propositions, indeed of propositions that reason is unable to accommodate. The response of faith is contrasted with knowledge in the involvement of the will—again an echo of Aquinas.[30] The involvement of the will in faith is analogous to its involvement in secular matters, such as our belief in the deliverances of the senses or in historical facts. Here, as the skeptic makes clear to us, we can never do more than approximate to the truth and have to leap beyond the available evidences to get to a conclusion. Kierkegaard indeed writes here of secular faith.[31] But in the case of religious faith, the leap is far more radical because the conclusion exceeds, indeed is contrary to, reason. So although in both the secular and the religious case he writes of faith as due to an act of will, he follows Aquinas again in saying that the will's act in the religious case is not one we can make on our own account but is due to the grace of God.

If we have been enabled to make it, however, what is our state of mind? One can here only quote the famous statement "Here is such a definition of truth: holding fast to an objective uncertainty in an appropriation process of the most passionate inwardness is the truth, the highest truth available for an existing individual." This is not the place for detailed exegesis. It is perhaps enough to indicate that "truth" is being used here not as a synonym for "fact" but as the name for the believer's state of mind and that (in a way once again remarkably reminiscent of Aquinas) this state of mind is being characterized as holding fast, or being certain, of something that is "objectively" uncertain. Our power to do this is being ascribed to an act of will that is due to God and not ourselves. Faith is being certain of what is uncertain by the standards of science or philosophy.[32]

The Decline of Foundationalism

In the preceding historical comments I have tried to show how the foundationalist programs of modern epistemology have affected thinking about faith. I have avoided the suggestion that the arguments of natural theology have depended on these programs. Since it has often been said in recent years that the defense of faith must be separated from foundationalist assumptions, it is important to notice briefly how and why those assumptions have declined in influence.

In the broadest terms most philosophers would now agree that once the egocentric predicament is agreed to be a real one, it cannot be escaped and that the circularity that besets the Cartesian attempt to escape it besets other attempts equally. However, many would deny that it is indeed a real one. For me to know I have conscious states, as Descartes holds, I have to be able to identify and name them, and it is commonly maintained that the capacity to do so is available only to members of a linguistic community whose reality Cartesian skepticism is supposed to place in doubt. Within that community the actual practice of reason in the sciences and common life does not follow the Cartesian model of inference from starting points that are certain. In fact, there are many distinct and autonomous forms of rationality, and it is merely chauvinistic to suppose that the deductive model of inference, or any other single model, must apply to all of them. Skepticism about any one of them is hard to express from within it and is arbitrary and groundless if advanced from outside. Philosophy must leave them as they are and cannot dictate to the forms of life and thought that it examines.

The greatest single influence in the development of these common attitudes is the work of Wittgenstein. He did not have a great deal to say himself about the philosophy of religion, and his influence on it has taken three distinct (and incompatible) forms. Some of those influenced by him have suggested that religious belief is incoherent. This criticism, and the attempts to answer it, dominated analytical philosophy of religion for many years in midcentury. A second form of influence is seen in the work of those who have argued, in ways that seem much closer to the intent of Wittgenstein's own remarks, that the religious form of life is coherent and autonomous and needs no external justification but that this can be recognized only if it is given a nonrealist interpretation in which traditional questions of truth cannot be raised. These concerns with the meaning of religious discourse have recently given place to a concern with the epistemology of religious conviction that reflects Wittgenstein's influence through a recognition of the autonomy and rationality of distinct forms of life without adopting a nonrealist interpretation of religious conviction. It is this third development that concerns us the most in the latter parts of this book.[33]

Notes

1. See Frankfort 1949; and Cornford 1957.

2. "And I desire that Nicanor, as he has been preserved, will perform the vow which I made on his behalf, and dedicate some figures of animals in stone, four cubits high, to Jupiter the saviour, and Minerva the saviour, in Stagira." Diogenes Laertius 1853, 186.

3. See Hatch 1957; Cochrane 1940; Nock 1965; Gilson 1941; and Mascall 1949, Chapter 1.

4. Tertullian (ca. 160–ca. 220) is famous for his question "What has Athens to do with Jerusalem?" and for his paradoxical claim that the very absurdity of core Christian claims is a reason for accepting them. For a brief comment on Tertullian, see, for example, Pelikan 1971, 49f. The intertwining of philosophical thought with Christian life and doctrine is celebrated and exemplified in Vesey 1989.

5. A helpful account of Augustine on faith is to be found in Chapter 3 of Pojman 1986. On Augustine's critique of skepticism, see Augustine 1943; and the essay by Kirwan in Burnyeat 1983.

6. Anselm 1903, 7. For a detailed discussion of the Ontological Argument, see Hick and Magill 1967.

7. This account of Thomas's analysis of faith is inevitably very compressed. I attempt a fuller treatment in Penelhum 1989. For an importantly different account, see Stump 1989. Thomas's analysis of faith is to be found primarily in two places: the first seven Questions of the Secunda Secundae (Part Two of Part Two) of the *Summa Theologiae* (Aquinas 1974) and Question 14 of De Veritate (On Truth) (Aquinas 1952).

8. *Summa Theologiae,* Part One Question One, Article 8, answer to second objection.

9. "To believe is an act of mind assenting to the divine truth by virtue of the command of the will as this is moved by God through grace; in this way the act stands under the control of free will and is directed towards God. The act of faith is, therefore, meritorious." ST IIaIIae 2,9 (Aquinas 1974, 97).

10. The Vatican Decrees of 1870, for example, refer to the miracles and prophecies as "most certain proofs" of divine revelation. These decreases are conveniently available as an appendix to MacGregor 1958; see particularly p. 155.

11. IIaIIae 6,2.

12. See James 2:19.

13. IIaIIae 5,2; Aquinas 1974, 153–157.

14. Stump 1989 thinks the latter, but I do not find the text as clear as this.

15. IIaIIae 2,2.

16. The best known of Luther's own statements about faith and its saving power is his treatise "The Freedom of a Christian" (1957). See Penelhum 1989, 37–46; and Swinburne 1981, 110–115.

17. First Meditation. See Descartes 1966, 61.

18. The authority on whom our present understanding of the role of skepticism in early modern philosophy depends is Richard Popkin. See Popkin 1979, 1980, 1993. On Skeptic thought in antiquity see Stough 1969; Burnyeat 1982, 1983; Annas and Barnes 1985; and Groarke 1990. On Descartes and skepticism, see also Curley 1978; and Williams 1978.

19. Sextus Empiricus 1933.

20. See Popkin 1979, Chapters 1–3. For a study of Montaigne, see Hallie 1966.

21. See Hookway 1990, Chapters 3–4.

22. De Santillana 1955.

23. Clarke 1978.

24. For a detailed treatment of the argument in Thomas's version, see Kenny 1969, 96–120.

25. See *Natural Theology* in vol. 1 of Paley 1838. See also Hurlbutt 1965.

26. Locke 1958, 1959.

27. The standard edition of Hume's *Dialogues* is that of Norman Kemp Smith (Hume 1947); an excellent recent edition is that of John Gaskin (Hume 1993). On Kant's philosophy of religion, see Webb 1926.

28. On Skeptical fideism, see Penelhum 1983.

29. The fragment containing it is 418 in the Lafuma ordering and 233 in the ordering of Leon Brunschvicg.

30. On this point, see Pojman 1984, Chapter 3.

31. Kierkegaard 1985, 72–88.

32. Kierkegaard 1941a, 182.

33. The indispensable volume for the study of the first form of Wittgensteinian criticism of religion is Flew and MacIntyre 1955; for the second, nonrealist interpretation of the religious form of life, see Phillips 1965, 1970, 1988; Winch 1967; and Keightley 1976.

CHAPTER THREE

Belief and the Will

"Now I'll give you something to believe. I'm just one hundred and one, five months and a day." *"I can't believe that,"* said Alice. *"Can't you?"* the Queen said in a pitying tone. *"Try again: draw a long breath, and shut your eyes."* Alice laughed. *"There's no use trying,"* she said: *"one can't believe impossible things."* *"I daresay you haven't had much practice,"* said the Queen. *"When I was your age, I always did it for half-an-hour a day. Why, sometimes I've believed as many as six impossible things before breakfast."*[1]

—Lewis Carroll

Some of the key players in the debate about faith, such as Aquinas and Kierkegaard, have said that believing (or at least religious believing) is an act of the will, that it is freely done. Although Aquinas maintains it is a rational act, he connects its freedom (and hence its merit) with the fact that belief falls short of knowledge. Kierkegaard goes much further, insisting not only that what the person of faith believes is objectively uncertain but also that it is in key respects paradoxical or contrary to reason. Both say that in faith, beliefs are held with psychological certainty. So faith involves being certain about that which is uncertain or, even, as the White Queen says, impossible.

These two very different thinkers also agree in ascribing the believer's ability to believe uncertain or impossible things to the special grace of God. In part this is because each sees faith as an example of what theologians call the paradox of grace: that is, the doctrine that whenever we manage to achieve anything acceptable to God, what looks from the outside like an action of ours is in fact due to special divine intervention. This teaching originates with Saint Paul, who tells us that what he and his fellow followers of Christ do is not attributable to them but to the Spirit of God within them.[2] But there is more at work here. It only makes sense to talk of something's being done miraculously if it makes sense to talk of its being done at all, and if what the White Queen says we can do with practice is something that it is absurd to suppose anybody does, then it is also absurd to suppose we could do it with divine help.

But what exactly *is* absurd in what the White Queen says she used to do? There would seem to be two candidates for the answer, not just one: believing to order and believing what is impossible. It is not clear what "impossible" means here. Peter Heath, in his edition of Lewis Carroll, argues that Alice should only class logically absurd propositions as impossible.[3] There have been quite a number of people who have been a hundred and one years old, so perhaps that is not impossible, merely unlikely. But the context makes it clear that the Queen would be undeterred by logic and thinks that practice would enable us to believe logically impossible things as well as merely unlikely ones. I begin with the question of how far it is possible to believe to order, or on command, and turn later to the special issues raised by paradox or logical impossibility.

Choosing to Believe

Philosophical examination of belief has tended to concentrate, not on the question before us, but on the issue first raised systematically by Plato in the *Theaetetus,* that of the relationship between belief and knowledge. But the one issue leads naturally, indeed inevitably, into the other. For knowledge is commonly seen as the attainment of a relationship to truth that we have not quite reached in the case of mere belief, even if the belief we have is true. Behind the attempt at defining this relationship is often an attempt to find a way of transforming beliefs so that they become knowledge or replacing them so that we have knowledge instead. This raises questions of how beliefs should be formed, abandoned, or replaced. These issues, sometimes referred to today as questions of doxastic ethics, imply views about how far we have the ability to control what we believe and how far not.

These philosophical issues have informal counterparts in the popular culture, especially in discussions of religion. Unbelievers think that those who have faith are credulous, that is, that they believe too easily. Believers think that their critics willfully disregard obvious truths about themselves and their world and so are perversely skeptical. Anthony Kenny defines rationality as the mean between credulity and skepticism.[4] Opinions of this sort embody judgments about how others have formed their beliefs and how they should reform their habits.

These opinions have not had very much direct philosophical treatment. Those philosophers who have discussed them have divided into those who think that believing is something that we do and those who think it is something that happens to us. The former group, whom we may call the voluntarists, think that we have voluntary control over what we believe in the way in which we have voluntary control over our actions. The latter group, whom we could (with less precedent) call the involuntarists, deny that we can choose whether to believe something because belief is not an action and therefore cannot be commanded or done to order.

There is another controversy about belief that overlaps this one in an untidy way: whether belief is an inner mental event or occurrence or whether it is a disposition or state. On the face of it, the former view seems to fit more easily with voluntarism, and the latter with involuntarism. Since I do not explore this question here, I merely say that the two controversies must be kept distinct. Hume, for example, is very clearly an involuntarist, but the account of belief that he gives assumes it to be an introspectible mental occurrence. Aquinas, who suggests that secular belief, or *opinio*, is a disposition, nevertheless talks about *credere*, the belief we have in faith, as an act that is the inner counterpart of the outer act of confession.

The language we use to talk about our beliefs is bewildering in ways it would not be if either voluntarism or involuntarism were clearly true. We do talk about preferring to believe one thing rather than another, of being inclined to believe one thing and also another, and of finding it difficult to believe this and easy to believe that. These idioms suggest that believing is, like an action, something that we choose, that our choice is often influenced by our desires, and that it may be either easy or difficult to carry it out. But we do not seem to follow this understanding consistently. We may well say, for example, that the alternative to the belief that we prefer is a proposition that we cannot believe rather than saying merely that we find it hard to do so. But even if we do say that we find it hard, we are not likely to suggest that believing it in the face of obstacles is an accomplishment for which we expect praise. On the contrary, the beliefs that we are proudest to have are beliefs that we often say no one can deny. An inability to do the opposite is something we offer as an excuse when we are discussing our actions, but it is something we point to with pride when we are talking about our beliefs. Perhaps this does not show that beliefs are not actions, but it at least shows that they are actions with an unusual logic.

We speak of our beliefs as being influenced by our desires; we also talk about being inclined to believe; and we say we believe things for reasons, just as we act for reasons. In the sphere of action, desires and inclinations may constitute the reasons for what I do, but they may also be temptations, and when I act, I may yield to them or resist them. But in spite of these analogies, the voluntarist view of belief runs into its greatest difficulties when their details are explored.

Classing beliefs as actions looks most plausible when we concentrate on those occasions when we "do not know what to believe" and have to cogitate and reflect in order to make up our minds. The analogy with action is closest here because we often have to deliberate between two courses of action to see what we should do. We may even reinforce the analogy by saying we are trying to decide what we should believe, thus appearing to bring in the concepts of prudence or obligation. But it is precisely here that the assimilation of belief and action breaks down.

In the first place, it is a notorious fact about human nature that when I have concluded, beyond all doubt, what I should do, I may fail to do it and do the opposite or do nothing. This is known as weakness of will, and however one tries to analyze it, we are all familiar with it. But there is no analog in the case of belief formation. When I have concluded what I should believe, there is not some additional step, called believing, that I still have to take. There is nothing left to do. If I know what I have to do in the sphere of action, I still have to perform the action and may not. But if I know what I must believe, I believe it already.

This prompts an objection: Are there not occasions when we say something like, "I know that everything points to p being true, but I just cannot bring myself to accept p"? Indeed, there are such occasions, and they need to be analyzed. But in spite of the wording, they are not occasions where we balk at going on to do something we know we ought to do. There is not some further step that remains to be taken. For if there were, it would be appropriate, and sometimes sufficient, just to say that we need to summon firmness and resolution, or some other phrase that the White Queen might use, and these are manifestly out of place.

We can see this difference better by noticing another. In the sphere of action we often face deadlines. We have to act by a certain time: We must vote tomorrow or not at all or accept the job offer by next Monday, or it will pass to another candidate. There may be many more things we would like to know or consider, but we cannot wait for them. But the same is not true about the formation of beliefs. For what happens when we vote, or act on the job offer, is that we act on what may well be incomplete information because we must. The nearest analog in the case of beliefs is the adoption of hypotheses or theories for the purpose of proceeding further in our inquiry even when the evidence does not conclusively support them. But it is not a matter of *believing* such hypotheses, though when we do adopt them in this way, we are more inclined to believe them than to believe the alternatives to them. Life often forces actions from us, but it does not force beliefs from us.

Here again an objection seems natural: Are there not many things about which it is unnatural to hesitate, so that only the skeptic doubts them? This is indeed so, but it is not because those who are not skeptics are forced to decide in favor of those beliefs by their circumstances. These are rather matters on which no one but philosophers has ever reflected. When we do reflect and are not in possession of conclusive information, beliefs are not forced from us, though decisions may be.

So although some forms of speech suggest that believing can be classed as a form of action, there is good reason to resist such a classification. But this does not show that beliefs are not, at least sometimes, the *products* of actions. A headache is not an action but may be the product of actions such as watching television or drinking. Similarly, even if a belief is not an action, it may arise as a result of actions such as looking through telescopes, considering clues, or reading newspapers. For this reason we may be responsible for having the beliefs we do, at least in some cases, just as we are sometimes to blame for the headaches we have. For the same reason we may trace our beliefs, directly or indirectly, to desires or fears because these may prompt actions that lead to beliefs. My fear of an enemy may prompt the inquiries that generate beliefs about his financial history that help me discredit him, for example. (This, however, is not the whole story about desire and belief, as we shall see.)

We can return now to the question of what is absurd about the White Queen's recollections about the beliefs of her childhood. We do not, in the first instance, have to be concerned with the fact that she says she used to believe things that are impossible; unlikely things will also manifest the absurdity of what she recalls. It seems clear, however, that whatever the absurdity is, it is not present in the case of believing *likely* things. At least it seems acceptable to say that I can believe all of the following six things before breakfast: that it is 7:30, that it is raining, that it is Monday, that I shall be late, that I shall think about philosophy before lunch, that there is breakfast waiting for me in the kitchen. Of course, in these cases there seems no reason to talk about having to try hard in order to believe them or to suppose I cannot believe them all at the same time. That is because whether true or false, they are all very likely. That, in turn, is obviously because in each case there is some uninterestingly obvious ground or evidence for them. In the case of something unlikely, the evidence will be against it. So when the Queen supposes that we need to make an effort and practice believing the unlikely things, she is supposing that the evidence I have, or the reasons I may have, are *obstacles* to believing that I have to surmount or disregard. That means that she thinks of believing as something I can do in some direct way just by trying to. The implied suggestion is that believing is like standing up or raising my arm or walking: These are all things that (unless I am specially handicapped) I can do just by deciding to do them. I had to learn them in infancy, and if I want to do them particularly well (to march on parade, say, or to dance on stage), I have to practice them and improve them. They are what philosophers have called basic actions that require, at most, concentration and effort.[5]

The Queen thinks of beliefs in the same way and consequently supposes the negative evidence against beliefs to be an obstacle analogous to stiffness in the joints when one wants to walk or the height of the bar when one wants to jump. One has only to summon up one's strength to overcome them or put them to one side and get on with—believing. But the nature of the absurdity of this view becomes clear when one imagines oneself faced with a command to believe and asks, "How?" After all, if one considers what happens when the evidence is all favorable, it is manifestly wrong to suggest that one could assemble the day's complement of needful beliefs more efficiently just by bypassing the consideration of all the evidence and getting on with believing the conclusions it points to. So one cannot command beliefs or decide to believe directly.

But this conclusion does not seem quite right either. For three very important and familiar facts stare us in the face. First, we all seem to have numberless beliefs that we have acquired without reflecting or considering evidence. Most of our beliefs, including the ones that obsess epistemologists, are in this category. Even though it is odd to "just try" to have this or that belief, or to command, we nevertheless seem just to *have* many beliefs. Second, we seem to ascribe many of the beliefs that *other people* have to their desires: They believe these things because they want to believe them. So we have the strange situation that, although we cannot, it seems, acquire beliefs just by trying to, we (or at least they) frequently do it just by wanting to. Can we make coherent sense of this situation? Third, although I hope to have done something to show the oddity of telling someone to believe, this is in fact something that many people urge on us all the time. Some evangelists tell us to believe and insist it is a necessary condition of our salvation. For some years I had on my desk a pamphlet on the front cover of which was the simple command "Stop doubting and believe." I have long since lost the pamphlet, but I am sure that the inside of it did not consist of instructions on how to go about fulfilling this command. It was much more likely to have consisted of reasons the reader should do what it said and the beneficial consequences of doing so. For one quite common element in the evangelists' repertoire is the subsidiary advice that if the hearer just *tries* believing, his or her life will be transformed. If it is absurd to command or urge anyone to believe, then how is it that evangelists go on saying things like this and that some of their hearers seem clearly to end up believing the very things they have been urged to believe? These difficulties are, I think, answerable. The answers to them leave us with a view of belief and its relation to the will that is a fairly conventional one among those contemporary philosophers who consider this matter.

Unconsidered Beliefs

When students of philosophy begin the theory of knowledge, they come to realize that they have many unacknowledged beliefs that it seems ludicrous to question but that epistemologists tell them they should try to justify in order to answer the skeptics. Regardless of whether such justifications can be had, these beliefs clearly are not acquired originally because we reflected on the justifications philosophers offer for them once skeptical questions are raised. The search for foundations in philosophy is largely the search for justifications for beliefs that it is unnatural to question. Descartes fully recognized this but thought it necessary to find such justifications if we are to attain to knowledge and not abandon all our beliefs to the skeptic. Controversies have raged since over the status of these natural, or commonsense, beliefs. Hume, for example, emphasized that they are not due to reasoning but to the instinctive dimensions of human personality, that, as he put it, "belief is more properly an act of the sensitive, than of the cogitative part of our natures."[6] He refrained from saying that we know these beliefs to be true but maintained that we have no choice but to accept them. G. E. Moore insisted that we do indeed know many of them to be true.[7] Wittgenstein emphasized that at least some of the key beliefs we have are inescapable and stressed the necessary role of authority in their origin and the impossibility of abandoning them, even in the process of questioning and doubt, since some have to be assumed when others are questioned.[8] In spite of obvious disagreements, all three take it for granted that most of the beliefs whose status concerns philosophers are beliefs that philosophers find already there. They argue about whether these beliefs can or should be endorsed, rejected, or replaced by philosophical means.

If beliefs are found by philosophers for the most part and not generated by their arguments, we can inquire not only about their justification but also about how they have come to be. Beliefs have what Hume called a natural history. So even if we cannot have beliefs to order, it is quite possible that we can have some degree of indirect control over them by choosing whether to set that history in motion.

What sets beliefs going and what does not seem to be an empirical matter, but obviously many of the causes that generate beliefs are actions that we can choose to do or not to do. We can choose whether to read books, attend lectures, look through microscopes, or ask awkward questions. All these may lead to the addition or subtraction of beliefs. However, tossing a coin, while it is sometimes the only way of making a decision, is no way at all of acquiring a belief. But since many of the things that lead to beliefs are things that we can do, beliefs are indirectly under our control, and we can be praised or blamed for many of our beliefs because we can be praised or blamed for the actions that lead to them. We can also, for the same reason, be praised or blamed for *not* having beliefs: I can be praised for having no opinion about my neighbor's marital life because I could have formed one only by prying into matters that should not concern me, and I can be blamed for having no opinion about the current election because I ought to take the trouble to read the papers.

So there can be doxastic ethics: prudential and moral rules about how to affect our processes of belief formation. We can view many epistemological theories as contributions to this. In "Rules for the Direction of the Mind," Descartes set out twenty-one methodological procedures for arriving at "solid and true judgments."[9] But we must be careful here. It is natural for philosophers to assume that any rules covering the formation of beliefs will be rules that lead, as Descartes says, to truth. We may perhaps allow, or even encourage, procedures that cause other people to have false beliefs: We might think it better that a dying patient be encouraged to believe he or she will recover or that a child be allowed to believe in Santa Claus. If we think so, it is because we think that sometimes it is more important to preserve peace of mind in the dying or to enrich childhood than to seek for truth. But when it comes to our own beliefs, we claim to be more single-minded and to think it reprehensible to follow procedures that are likely to lead to anything other than truth in our beliefs. We do admit some exceptions to this, of course. We may well think it right and proper to tell ourselves, in the teeth of experience, that we can run a mile in four and a half minutes or be back at our desks two days after succumbing to the flu. So we do sometimes think it is prudentially or morally good to set processes of belief formation going, in ourselves and in others, with objectives other than the pursuit of truth. But if this is sometimes the right thing to do, when is it, and when is it not? This is a very hard question, alien to most academic philosophers, who labor in a context where truth is assumed to be the only acceptable objective.

So there can be doxastic ethics because beliefs have natural histories that we can control or influence, and when we begin to consider what doxastic rules we should follow, we are sometimes forced to weigh the pursuit of truth in the balance against other goods. But however we judge their relative weight, we have to recognize another fact of great importance: Here, as elsewhere, our influence is limited. The philosopher who most clearly understood this, and thought longest and hardest about its implications, was Hume. The beliefs that the philosophical skeptic makes us doubt are, Hume tells us, beliefs that are not the result of reasoning; but the skeptic's reasoning can make us anxious about them. Fortunately this anxiety does not last long, not because the skeptic's reasonings have been satisfactorily answered (they have not), but because the nonintellectual forces in human nature that have generated those beliefs in the first place are far too strong for the skeptic's cavils to overcome. Nature is too strong for him, and we are lucky that it is. Reason can at most modify and refine (as Hume says, methodize and correct) beliefs that we are, in twentieth-century language, programmed to have. Hume did not (or did not altogether) think that religious beliefs were immovable in this way because he thought that their causes were environmental and social and did not lie deep in our natures. He believed that their natural history was of the kind that we could influence.[10] But regardless of whether he was correct about this, Hume's thought makes clear to us that when we try to influence the formation of our beliefs, we may find that we cannot do so as effectively as we would like, that our favored method of belief formation or modification may fail to generate, alter, or eliminate beliefs as we think it should. A belief that we acquired in a way that does not now meet with our favor may persist. However much we may realize that our belief in the dangerousness of walking under ladders has disreputable origins, we may be unable to rid ourselves of the anxiety we feel when we approach a ladder placed over the sidewalk, though of course we can maintain our pace and walk under it as resolutely as we like.

Belief and Desire

Beliefs, then, have a natural history, and we may find when we explore that natural history that the factors that generate our beliefs entrench them in ways that make it hard for philosophical or scientific reasoning to dislodge them. Among these nonratiocinative causes of belief are our passions and desires and the influence of habit and convention.

Although Hume and Pascal were opposite in so many respects, they both saw and emphasized the extent to which our beliefs are generated and influenced by these factors.[11] Both were unimpressed by the claims of philosophers to provide foundations for the propositions of faith, and both recognized the extent to which social inclinations and customs militated against it. Hume thought this was desirable since faith was something he rejected, but Pascal encouraged the very "monkish virtues" that Hume despised because they turned one away from the blandishments of the world and made it easier to "listen to God." The essence of the Wager argument is the recommendation to control one's passions in the interest of coming to believe. The influence of company and society is recognized: One must associate with other believers and join with them in acting as though one believed already; then perhaps one will come to share the beliefs they have.

So we have two major thinkers who say, in opposite tones of voice, that our beliefs are deeply influenced by our passions and by our social habits and that reason has little power over them. They may be far too pessimistic in thinking this. There is no doubt that we live in an era when reasoning has had more influence over belief than it has ever had before. But there is also no doubt that the powers they thought have greater influence than reason has are indeed important and pervasive features of human nature. The fact that there are such things as intellectual fashions is enough to confirm that there are social causes for belief. But it would seem that if our beliefs are due to social causes, they are due, at one remove, to desires we have, in this case the desire for conformity, popularity, or notoriety.

We can now return to the matter of how far we can believe things merely because we want to believe them, in spite of the fact that it seems to make no clear sense to say that we can believe them just by trying to. Pascal, we must notice, does not suggest that we can believe in God just by wanting to; for although he argues that believing in God is something that would be in our interest, he sees the absence (or supposed absence) of good arguments for God's existence as a genuine barrier to belief, which would not be so if it were something we could do merely from desire. Although we do not always want what we see is in our interest, we often do; and he has his imaginary skeptic expressing a clear wish that he could believe. What he recommends are indirect ways of conditioning ourselves by habit and association so that we come to believe in God. So he, at least, does not think that we can come to believe merely by wanting to believe.

But does this not happen very commonly? We often say, certainly, that people believe things because they want to: I believe that my much-loved cousin's sudden financial windfall is due to hard work and good judgment, not embezzlement, or that my much-hated rival's windfall is due to embezzlement, not hard work and good judgment. The key to understanding these familiar situations is that they are, in spite of the phrasing, *not* examples of believing things because we want to believe them.[12]

The reason I believe my cousin's good luck is admirable is not, although we say it is, that I want to believe the best of him. The reason I believe my rival's good luck is discreditable is not, although we say it is, that I want to believe the worst of him. It is indeed true that my desires cause me to believe the best of my cousin and the worst of my rival. But the relevant desires are not the desires to believe anything. The desire that makes me believe the best of my cousin is the desire that the best be *true* of him: that his good fortune should indeed be due to his hard work and good judgment. The desire that makes me believe the worst of my rival is the desire that the worst be true of him: that *his* good fortune should be due to his criminality. These are powerful sorts of desires, and as far as the evidence goes, they are often quite strong enough to produce beliefs on their own, although they may also do so indirectly by making us seek out evidence in favor of what we hope is true and ignoring evidence that suggests what we hope is false. But they are not desires to *do* anything. They are desires for certain facts to obtain, and they cause us to believe sometimes that they do obtain. This phenomenon is often called wishful thinking. When it operates in the face of contrary available evidence, it may be something that is usually worse, namely, self-deception.[13]

We can summarize this segment of the argument as follows. Habit, convention, and desire all contribute to our deposit of beliefs, either directly or indirectly by affecting the direction and intensity of our intellectual activities. But this in no way shows that we should think of beliefs as actions, and in particular it does not help give sense to the suggestion that believing is something we can do to order. It is nevertheless important philosophically that beliefs we acquire through any of these nonratiocinative sources may be hard to dislodge, even when reasoning points to conclusions that are contrary to them. It is also important philosophically to note that what we cannot do directly we can sometimes do indirectly, and hence we can induce beliefs in ourselves (as we can induce them in others) not only by encouraging intellectual inquiry but also through association, habit, and persuasive devices.

"Just Believe!"

We have already seen that the idiomatic features of the language of belief are philosophically misleading. This is especially the case with the verbal forms of the urgings of evangelists. They appear to tell their hearers simply to believe and to be telling them to do this sometimes on the grounds that it is prudent to do so. If there is merit in the arguments we have just examined, this appearance must be deceptive, for it is not possible to believe just by trying to, however much one may wish one did. This does not mean, of course, that one cannot be urged to take steps that will lead to one's believing. Such scenarios are of several kinds.

1. The simplest, and the most likely to be the result of the crudest forms of evangelism, is the situation in which a hearer has already been partially persuaded of the likelihood that his or her eternal future is very dark if belief is not forthcoming. This scenario already involves a degree of belief in some of the propositions that form the content of the faith the evangelist is trying to promote. What is needed is the acceptance of the rest, for which, perhaps, the hearer feels there is no good evidence beyond the evangelist's insistence. In such a situation the hearer may feel it prudent to engage in steps that will, he or she hopes, lead to belief. Such steps may consist of a detailed consideration of the positive evidence, to which the hearer may now turn with a renewed sense of urgency. This is the evangelistic strategy that we find in the superficially dry pages of Butler's *The Analogy of Religion,* where readers assumed to agree on the existence of God are urged to reconsider the claims of the Christian revelation on the grounds of their importance.[14] However, the steps the intending believer takes may consist merely in the hopeful performance of the acts of contrition and surrender

that would be forthcoming if he or she really believed already; these may be undertaken to induce the inner state of which they are the natural manifestation—especially if they are undertaken in the company of others who are judged already to be true believers.

2. A similar but distinct scenario is the one envisioned by Pascal in his Wager argument.[15] Here the hearer is assumed to be moved wholly by prudential considerations and to have no prior inclination toward belief otherwise. The believing wager is one in which the hearer, unable to tell through reason what the cosmic truth is, nevertheless can see that the losses that would be caused by unbelief if God does exist are infinitely greater than those that would be caused by belief if he does not. Pascal assumes the hearer to be skeptical about reason's capacity to arrive at truth about God but not to have reached the stage of indifference about our place in the cosmos that the classical Skeptic affected. It is not unlikely that many who hear evangelists are in mental positions like that of Pascal's imagined interlocutor, even though they may be innocent of the technical refinements of skepticism. If this is so, then since reason has not produced any prior inclinations toward belief, any belief that results will be due to nonratiocinative devices: attending religious ceremonies, associating with believers, and the like. Here it is belief itself that is targeted, and these performances are undertaken to induce it. It is notable that Pascal stresses that they include the adoption of habits that will reduce those forms of attachment to worldly pleasures that he supposes make us wish the claims of the faith to be untrue.

3. Pascal's recognition that passions and desires hinder belief by making us want the faith to be false can lead us to a third scenario of response to evangelism.[16] He is exceptionally vitriolic about the skeptic's habit of indifference toward questions he cannot answer;[17] and Pascal has a very negative perception of the human love of games and play, which he sees as self-deceiving distractions from those aspects of our condition that, when recognized, would make us want to listen to God.[18] Because of these features of his evangelistic strategy, Pascal is often considered by unbelievers to be a sour and life-denying figure.[19] His strategy, and that of hosts of other evangelists who are of lesser sophistication, is often judged to be based on the appeal to fear. But if Pascal seeks to make us cease wanting the claims of religion to be false and to start wanting them

to be true by showing us what he judges to be the defects of our
condition, others preach by presenting a vision of the world that
they hope will so enamor us that we will wish it to be the true one.
These are the evangelists of the more mystical and visionary persuasion. Their strategy is eloquently described by Newman:

> The Word of Life is offered to a man; and, on its being offered, he
> has faith in it. Why? On these two grounds—the word of its human
> messenger, and the likelihood of the message. And why does he feel
> the message to be probable? Because he has a love for it, his love be-
> ing strong, though the testimony is weak. He has a keen sense of the
> intrinsic excellence of the message, of its desirableness, of its likeness
> to what it seems to him Divine Goodness would vouchsafe did He
> vouchsafe any, of the need of a Revelation, and its probability.[20]

The last three words prevent this passage from reflecting our particular perception of the evangelist's strategy unmixed with other factors, but it is still clear that the primary moving force in that strategy, as Newman presents it, is that of showing the hearer the
"excellence" of the message—that is, making him or her want it to
be true because it would be supremely good. This coincidence of
the content of faith with the object of the hearer's desire for the
good (rather than for the expedient or the safe) is key to Aquinas's
distinction between formed and unformed faith, formed faith being
the outcome of assent that is determined not only by signs or evidences but also by a love of God as the supreme good.[21] This scenario is one in which the hearer comes to believe in whole or in part
because he or she perceives the propositions of the faith as good in
themselves. Belief comes, not because *belief* is wanted (as in our
second scenario), but because what comes to be believed in is
wanted.

These three scenarios are not the only possible ones, and it is ar-
tificial to separate them. But they are ways in which the evangelist's
command to believe can be understood without resorting to the absurd view of the White Queen that belief can be commanded. In
each the evangelist seeks to activate, or to get the hearer to activate,
nonratiocinative factors that are likely to lead to belief. When understood in this way, the command to believe can indeed make
sense and be followed, and any belief that results can be explained.

Of course, all these forms of strategy are open to criticism. My
use of the cumbersome adjective "nonratiocinative" to describe the

factors they activate is deliberate, since at this point I do not wish to comment on the criticisms that philosophers are likely to make. But many would simply describe these factors as "nonrational" or even "irrational." The first strategy is often thought to be immoral because it is said to depend on fear, the second is condemned because it is thought to be immoral to base beliefs on anything other than available evidence, and the third looks to many like nothing better than an appeal to wishful thinking. These are all condemnations that presuppose certain principles in doxastic ethics that I discuss later. For the present it is enough to recognize that our power to induce and sustain beliefs in others and in ourselves is, it seems, always a matter of choosing procedures, intellectual or other, that bring beliefs about and reinforce them.

Believing the Impossible

The White Queen did not merely say that she had practiced believing for half an hour a day and had managed to believe six things. She also said they were *impossible* things. She did not distinguish clearly between very unlikely things and logically absurd ones. Those who have faith quite often say that the things they believe are amazing and not to have been expected, even though they think they are true. Only a small minority insist they are absurd. Even Pascal does not say this, though Kierkegaard seems to, and Tertullian is notorious for having done so.

We are all quite at ease in saying of others that they believe things we know to be false, even logically absurd. But radical fideists such as Kierkegaard or Tertullian seem willing, indeed eager, to say this about themselves and the beliefs that they have: That is, they seem to insist that what they themselves believe is contrary to reason. Is the state of mind they claim to represent a possible one; and if it is not, what state of mind is it that they are mistakenly describing in this way? Our previous discussions of belief, will, and reason have equipped us to answer this question.

One result of the fact that beliefs are so often present in us as a result of training or of desire is the fact that later education or reflection leads us to believe things that are inconsistent with beliefs we already have from such causes. Indeed, the inner conflict that results from this inconsistency is one of the primary sources of philosophy. Skeptical philosophers make some of these beliefs explicit and show us that there are reasons against them, for example, thus leading to the epistemology of sense perception; or reflection on the foundations of scientific explanation generates philosophical anxiety about the assumption of freedom that we make when praising or blaming each other. However, we sometimes have beliefs we arrived at through careful, even expert, reflection challenged by the impact of our emotions. Revulsion against laissez-faire economic wisdom has frequently owed its power to sympathy for the victims of untrammeled capitalism. In these cases we are faced with a lessening of the power of beliefs when those beliefs are challenged by information that is inconsistent with them or by their collision with our passions or desires.

The description of these conflict states is difficult to articulate and difficult to interpret once achieved. One common way of describing them is to say that a belief we once had is now one we hold less strongly and that we are doubtful about it. Another common way is to say that we used to hold one belief but are now undecided between it and some other belief that is incompatible with it. When we speak in these ways, we appear to assume that we are not able to hold two incompatible beliefs (that is, the belief that p and the belief that not-p or the belief that p and the belief that q, which we know entails not-p) at the same time. Our criteria of rationality seem to depend on this assumption: A rational person is a person who has doubts about a belief when the evidence suggests it is false and who is undecided between two beliefs when there are grounds for each and both cannot be true.

One reason for the appeal of voluntarist views of belief comes from this assumption, as we have seen. But I have argued earlier that when we see that the grounds point to a particular conclusion, we have no further step to take toward believing that conclusion but do it already. If this argument is sound, it seems to follow that on at least some of these complicated occasions of inner conflict about belief, we must have two inconsistent beliefs at one time. The causes or reasons for our holding one of them have not gone away, and so the belief itself has not; but we find that we nevertheless have come, again either through reasons or through causes, to have another belief that is incompatible with the first.[22] When we are involved in such a conflict of beliefs, what can we do? One thing we can do is engage in what is called compartmentalization: attending to one of the beliefs on Mondays, Wednesdays, and Fridays and the other on Tuesdays, Thursdays, and Saturdays. Another is concentrating on the more attractive of the two beliefs and hoping that the other will wither away. A third is resolutely acting on the one in order to weaken the grip of the other. (This is how hardy souls fight their superstitions—by walking under every threatening ladder and spilling salt on purpose.) But what does a *rational* person do?

That depends on what a rational person is. We can certainly follow Anthony Kenny and say that rationality in belief is the mean between credulity and skepticism. But that does not tell us how to strike that balance. Some think it obvious that if a belief we have acquired through a consideration of evidence collides with one we have acquired through upbringing or instinct, we should resolve the conflict by doing everything we can to undermine the latter. This would be a special application of the theory called evidentialism, which tells us that beliefs the rational person has should be based on evidence. But this theory is controversial: It is not self-evident that evidence is the only source of beliefs that is likely to lead to truth, let alone other objectives. Having said this, however, we must also notice that there is something obviously perverse about the suggestion that a conflict between a belief based on evidence and one incompatible with it can rationally be resolved in the opposite way: by undermining the evidence-based belief. It is rational, most would agree, when such a conflict arises, to go back to the evidence and reexamine it; but it is not rational to deal with conflict by nonintellectual devices and ignore the evidence one has.

It is here that the demands of rationality lead into philosophy. For the rational person is clearly someone who would try to resolve such conflict by assessing the credentials of the belief that is not due to evidence. To assess these credentials is to assess the power of the various nonevidential causes to lead us to truth. It is a notable feature of contemporary epistemological thought that it embraces many discussions of the truth-bearing value of testimony, tradition, feeling, and authority, to name a few. Classical foundationalism, following the lead of Descartes and Locke, has tended to regard these sources of belief as necessarily subordinate, for the rational person, to a priori reasoning and sense-perception. In different ways Hume, Reid, and Wittgenstein have made many epistemologists question this approach, not least by making clear to us how little able we are in practice to follow this standard. But the foundationalist position is still virtually unchallenged in one respect: that if beliefs we have from other causes collide with beliefs formed in the ways classical foundationalism approved, the latter can only give way in a rational person if there are good reasons to think that the causes with which they are colliding are also reliable sources of true belief.

The epistemological questions that are raised as soon as we ask which causes of belief are rationally dependable and which not are huge ones, to which I have made no contribution here whatever. I have merely argued that the determination of when it is, and when it is not, rational to resolve a conflict of belief in favor of a belief that is not based on evidence or reasoning is a determination that depends on the assessment of the kinds of cause that belief has. But all this seems to assume that we *want* to be rational. Does not the radical fideist question the legitimacy of this very desire? I wish now to argue that, although this may appear to be the case, what the fideist is doing is merely misrepresenting the nature of the conflict of beliefs to which he or she is responding.

I begin by quoting a lengthy statement of a radical fideist position. It does not come from Tertullian or Kierkegaard but from Pierre Bayle. Bayle, in his *Historical and Critical Dictionary* and many other writings, continually emphasizes the ways in which orthodox Christian doctrines collide with reason while maintaining that one must accept them nevertheless. His intentions are a matter of controversy, but I assume his sincerity here since what is at issue is not his private views but the coherence of the position he is presenting.[23] In Remark M to the *Dictionary* article on Spinoza, he tells of a Johannes Bredenbourg who sought to refute Spinoza and constructed a demonstration of some of Spinoza's main theses for himself in order to answer them. Bredenbourg then could find no defect in the demonstration. He was accused of atheism (as Spinoza was) but defended himself by appealing to the distinction between faith and reason. He argued that just as both Catholics and Protestants believe in the Trinity, though it is "inconsistent with the light of nature," so he believed in free will, even though reason could prove that everything happens by necessity. Bayle defends Bredenbourg as follows:

> One may cry out, that he is not sincere, and that our mind is not formed in such a manner, as to believe that true, which a geometrical demonstration shows to be false; but is this not erecting oneself into

a judge in a case where incompetency maybe objected to us? . . .
For it must be observed that there is no contradiction between
these two things: 1. The light of reason shows me that this is false, 2.
I believe it however, because I am persuaded that this light is not in-
fallible, and because I choose rather to submit to an inward sentiment, and the impressions of conscience, in short to the word of
God, than to a metaphysical demonstration. This is not at all the
same as believing and not believing the same thing at the same
time.[24] That combination is impossible, and no person ought to be
allowed to allege it for his justification. . . . The Abbé Dangeau
mentions certain persons who have religion in their mind, but not
in their heart. . . . I believe one can also say that there are people
who have religion in their heart, but not in their mind.[25] They lose
sight of it, when they seek it by the methods of human reasoning
. . . but when they leave off disputing and only attend to the inward
proofs, the instincts of conscience, the force of education, &c, they
are convinced of religion, and conform themselves to it as far as human infirmity permits.

Bayle paints a picture here of the fideistic believer choosing to
follow the heart rather than the head, just as in the sphere of action
one might choose to follow one mentor's advice rather than another's. But the sphere of believing is not the sphere of action. And,
most important, if one has judged a "geometrical demonstration"
to be conclusive, one cannot *then* elect not to believe its conclusion.
If, however, one also believes something inconsistent with it, either
from earlier "education" or from the later "instincts of conscience,"
the acceptance of the conclusion may very well not drive its competitor out. This happens frequently. In other words, it is entirely
possible, contrary to what Bayle says, that we can believe and not
believe a thing at the same time. We can, and do, suffer from a flat
conflict between two beliefs.

Has Bayle described one way in which a person can resolve such
a conflict? I have argued that a *rational* person would attempt to resolve the conflict in a way that gives a certain kind of preference to
the reasoned belief: either by trying to eradicate its competitor or
by discerning good epistemological credentials in the sources of the
competitor's presence, which would at least concede to the reasoned belief the right of an answer. But is Bayle not suggesting that
we can put rationality to one side in the interests of truth or at least
of "religion"?

Perhaps he is, and people do in fact behave in such ways. For example, to take a case that has some analogies with religion but is not itself religious, if I am confronted by very strong evidence that someone dear to me is guilty of a crime, I may well deny that evidence while knowing very well (as we say) that it is very strong. (Remember that Bayle and Kierkegaard write as though the negative evidence is conclusive.) We have a name for such responses; they are forms of self-deception. If I am right that someone who sees the conclusiveness of an argument does not then have a choice not to accept it, then if that person rejects it in the interest of a conflicting belief, that person is rejecting something that he or she knows very well and is guilty of self-deception. Bayle compounds this self-deception by denying the reality of the conflict state of which it is a resolution. He denies it by supposing that the subject can choose *not to have* the reasoned belief, even while accepting the reasoning that generates it. In practice this may make the conflict tolerable by enabling the person who has it to pretend it is not there.

Of course, it is quite common for us to consider arguments and evidence and to resist them when we see that they point toward conclusions we dislike. We may raise objections to the inferences, insist on reexamining the evidence to unearth unnoticed flaws, uncover tacit assumptions, or make new distinctions. Philosophers and lawyers are trained to do these things. Such intellectual moves are not intrinsically self-deceiving. But they become so when the resistance is clearly unreasonable, as, for example, when we pretend we do not know things that we know perfectly well. It is hard to discern when reasonable caution ends and self-deception begins. The borderline between them is the limit of rationality. I have suggested that the stance of the radical fideist such as Bayle or Kierkegaard is on the far side of it.

An objection is still natural here. I have suggested that the radical fideist position denies the reality of a conflict of beliefs. But does Bayle not freely admit that there is a conflict between reason and the heart? Where is the self-deception? And if he is accused of irrationality, has he not already cheerfully pleaded guilty?

The answer to these questions is that Bayle's stance, through its implied misdescription of the logic of belief, involves him in denying the very presence of one of the two conflicting beliefs. It does this by conceding that its conclusion has been demonstrated by "geometrical reasoning" but saying he has decided not to accept it.

In saying that he chooses to believe what feeling tells him and reject what reason tells him, he is merely repressing, not excising, the reasoned conclusion. His verbal choice of feeling over reason entails a self-deceiving denial of the conflict that still continues within him as long as his consciousness of the import of the reasoning continues.

Self-deception is often successful. Those who deceive themselves about such doxastic conflicts may well emerge with only the belief dictated by feeling remaining. Then there is no conflict. But as long as the awareness of the strength of the case for its competitor remains, the conflict does also, and the radical fideist is in self-deception. Radical fideism poses to the world as a healthy, animal reaction to bloodless reason. To recognize the falsity of this pose, we need only remember that self-deception is a vice that requires high intelligence.

Some Tentative Conclusions

I have suggested that erecting the rejection of reason into a general principle entails self-deception about the state of one's beliefs. This does not mean that such causes as "inward sentiment and the impressions of conscience," to use Bayle's language, must always yield when they conflict with evidence or reasoning. It is the merit of much recent epistemology of religion to have made this clear. It is true that since radical fideism is not the mere rejection of the primacy of evidence and reasoning but a self-deceiving denial of epistemic conflict, more than a nominal negativity about evidence and reasoning is needed when such a clash comes about. But what rationality requires is that such conflict be resolved in a way that gives the victory to beliefs that are due to causes that are epistemically reliable over those that are not.

Since Descartes and Locke, philosophers have had narrow views about what causes of belief are epistemically reliable. If beliefs that have arisen from causes such as tradition, authority, religious experience, and even some desires conflict with those that are generated by reasoning and evidence, then unless one wishes to suggest that reasoning and evidence are unreliable sources of belief (that is, to lapse into skepticism), it is requisite that the resulting conflict be resolved in one of two ways. Either reasoning and evidence win, or a cause be shown for supposing that with regard to the subject matter of the beliefs in question, tradition, authority, religious experience, or even the relevant desire is a more reliable cause for believing. To assume this cannot be done is mere prejudice. To do it, however, is a hugely difficult task whose magnitude is only beginning to be appreciated.

Notes

1. Quoted in Heath 1974, 179–180.
2. See, for example, Galatians 2:20 and 1 Corinthians 15:10.
3. Heath 1974, 180.
4. Kenny 1992, 6.
5. Danto 1973, Chapter 2.
6. Hume 1978, 183.
7. See Moore 1959, 32–59.
8. Wittgenstein 1969.
9. Descartes 1966, 153.
10. See Hume 1957, 21.
11. Penelhum 1993.
12. The argument I present here is due to the important insight of Bernard Williams (1973), especially 149–151.
13. This remark is not offered as an analysis of self-deception. For a discussion, see Fingarette 1969.
14. Butler 1900, vol. 2, especially II 7.
15. Pascal 1966, fragment 418.
16. Ibid., fragment 12.
17. Ibid., fragment 427.
18. Ibid., fragments 132–139.
19. See, for example, the essay on Pascal in Huxley 1956.
20. Newman 1970, 202–203.
21. On this, see Stump 1989, 167–192.
22. I am inclined to think that when the conflict is between two beliefs that are both based on reasoning and reflection, it is less misleading to use idioms that imply we can have only one belief at a time and to say in consequence that we are undecided between two positions and for the present hold neither. The language of belief conflict, in which we can have two incompatible beliefs at once, is more clearly accurate for cases where one of the two beliefs is held without prior consideration of evidence or reasons and the other is the consequence of such consideration. But I do not know how to prove this.

23. Labrousse 1983; Bayle 1965. The material quoted here is taken from vol. 9 of the 1734 English translation of the *Dictionary*.

24. I am following Popkin's emendation here, as the 1734 translation is inaccurate.

25. Again I follow Popkin in correcting an omission in the 1734 English version.

CHAPTER FOUR

Faith, Certainty, and Anxiety

Faith and Knowledge

We have so far been examining some of the puzzles that arise from the fact that faith is thought to be a voluntary state, though belief does not seem to be something one chooses. I turn now to another puzzle. Writers as different as Aquinas and Kierkegaard seem to agree not only that faith is voluntary but also that it involves certainty without knowledge. The concept of certainty is ambiguous since the word can be used either to describe the state of mind of the person who believes or to indicate something of the epistemic status of the beliefs he or she has.[1] We may for convenience speak of subjective and objective certainty, the former being the subject's state of mind and the latter being the standing of the supposed truths believed in. Using this language, both Aquinas and Kierkegaard hold that in faith one has subjective certainty on matters that are objectively uncertain.[2]

From the outside this view of the nature of faith seems to be an obviously correct description of the way believers proceed. Although they may frequently use the language of knowledge, they may also willingly admit that the evidence they have would not convince all reasonable people. Even if believers do not concede this much, outsiders will commonly complain of just this combina-

tion, so that Aquinas and Kierkegaard seem merely to be acknowl-
edging a fact that critics of faith think is obvious.

As we have seen, there are other reasons for their position.
Aquinas makes very clear that the merit that makes faith a virtue
could be present in faith only if the believer has freedom in believing and that when there is knowledge (which he thinks comes only
from vision or from proof), there is no such freedom. Kierkegaard,
who sees the skeptic as choosing not to assent when others would,
sees the believer as choosing to say yes in the face of barriers that
deter those unblessed by grace: the source of his famous metaphor
of the "leap" of faith.

What reasoning of this sort does is to suggest a necessary connection between faith and objective uncertainty. If there were such
a connection, then it would provide both an argument against faith
and an argument that could be used to defend it. The argument
against faith would be that it is only rational to commit oneself
wholeheartedly when one is in a position to be sure of the truth.
The argument in defense of faith would be that if the evidence for
the faith looks inadequate, this is just what one should expect. What
merit is there, after all, in saying yes to what one cannot say no to? I
do not suggest these are sound arguments; they are not. But they
are obvious ones and often used.

I wish to argue that the relationship between faith and objective
uncertainty is not necessary. The best way to see this is to recall the
extent to which belief can be thought voluntary: A belief cannot be
directly commanded or chosen, but one can command or choose
some of the processes that may cause it. I cannot rid myself of a belief by mere choice either, though here, too, I can choose to initiate
processes that may weaken or destroy it. Given these possibilities, I
can acquire merit or demerit in the formation or elimination of beliefs, even though belief is not itself an action.

What is true of belief here is also true of knowledge. However
much I may think it good that I know something, I cannot know it
merely by choosing to, as any student knows. But I can initiate
processes that may lead to the knowledge I want to have. (This is
called learning!) I can be properly praised or blamed for what I
choose to acquire knowledge of and for what I choose to do to get
it. I can also be praised or blamed for what I choose not to know,
what I choose to shed my knowledge of, or what I allow myself to

forget; and I can be praised or blamed for whatever I choose to do that leads to these various consequences.

It is a matter of controversy in epistemology whether knowledge includes belief or whether it is a completely different state of affairs. Most philosophers hold the view that knowledge is true belief plus some other condition or conditions; Plantinga, who takes this view, calls the additional condition "warrant."[3] I do not need or wish to take a side here, although the issues on which I do wish to offer an opinion are relevant to it. I am arguing only that there are exact parallels between belief and knowledge in the area of the relation of each to the will and therefore to merit and demerit. If this argument is correct, it seems to follow that there is no reason deriving from these considerations for holding that faith and knowledge are exclusive. If those who have faith should be praised (or blamed) for holding certain propositions to be true, and if this praise (or blame) is justified because they have some degree of freedom in coming, or continuing, to hold these propositions, this justification should be unaffected by any decision on whether their holding these propositions to be true is a matter of knowledge or "mere" belief.

This does not show that faith and knowledge are *not* exclusive. But it certainly suggests that if they are, it is because the beliefs that are at the core of faith lack whatever characteristics would turn them into knowledge (or replace them by it).[4] This argument also suggests that if faith and knowledge are exclusive, this is a contingent matter about the ways the beliefs of the faithful are acquired, not a necessary feature of what it is to have faith or what it is to know or believe. So I proceed hereafter as though the exclusion has not been justified, even though I do not suppose I have demonstrated that it cannot be. I proceed, in other words, as though faith can include knowledge rather than mere belief: that is, that there is no reason in the discernible logic of faith that someone who has it should not *know* that what he or she confesses is true.

Since this will seem counterintuitive to some, I attempt to show that its consequences are not as radical as they may appear. It does not, in the first place, imply that any of those who have faith actually have knowledge, only that it is not absurd to suggest that they might have. Nor does it commit us to any view about what would make the believer's assent an instance of knowledge, if that ever occurs. This view does, however, allow us to concede that certain things *could* be true. One is that a religious believer may know *some* of the propositions to which he or she assents and merely believe others. Another is that the propositions in these two classes may shift, as life goes on, from one to the other and back again. Another is that some believers may know certain truths of the faith that other believers only believe—the major spiritual figures of a religious tradition may know some things that their disciples only believe, or the earlier members of the tradition only believe things that some later ones come to know. These consequences seem harmless and reasonable, and they conform to what believers think about their collective and individual experience.

A further result is that a common philosophical division between what is learned through reason and what is learned through revelation seems less obvious. Thomas says that, even though one person can know what another believes, one and the same person cannot both know and believe the same proposition at the same time. Thomas infers from this conclusion that those propositions about God that can be proved by reason are not properly classed as part of the faith, even though many only learn of them through revelation.[5] If faith can include knowledge as well as belief, there seems no reason to follow him in this. We can say that if there indeed were such a thing as successful natural theology, there would be no reason to exclude what it would prove to us from the body of the faith that it would support. (There might still be other reasons, of course, for thinking that not *all* the propositions of the faith could be made available in this way without special revelation.) These points are religiously neutral ones. They do not show that the claims of any faith are true or that anyone knows them to be if they are. They merely show that if anyone were indeed to know such things, he or she could still be part of the faith.

I return now to the matter of certainty and faith. If the present argument is true, we must reject the thesis that faith requires the combination of subjective certainty and objective uncertainty. The faith of many believers may indeed conform to this formula for anything we have said so far. But it is not necessary, for it to *be* faith, that it should so conform because objective uncertainty is not a condition of faith.

One reason that we often give to explain the confidence that a person has in a proposition that a critic questions is that, contrary to what the critic thinks, that person knows the proposition in question to be true. He knows that his friend is good for repayment on the loan because he has already received the check. She is confident that her child is safe after the accident because she has just had a phone call confirming this. So one result of not legislating that faith and knowledge are exclusive is that it becomes possible to defend the certainty of a believer as being the result of knowledge, at least sometimes. So even if faith entails subjective certainty, this does not have to be present in the face of objective uncertainty, though it may be. It is now time to ask how far subjective certainty is itself a requirement of faith, whatever the epistemic standing of the propositions the believer believes. This question requires a lengthier answer.

Faith and Belief

One of the most important classical texts on faith is Chapter 11 of the Letter to the Hebrews in the New Testament. Verses 5–6 tell us that Enoch had pleased God, "and without faith it is impossible to please him; for anyone who comes to God must believe that he exists and that he rewards those who search for him."[6] Most of the chapter consists in reminders of the great figures of Jewish history whose faith had pleased God; yet a hasty reading of this verse would easily suggest that faith consists simply in holding beliefs, primarily that in God's existence. The events the author writes of, however, make very clear that the faith of these figures consisted of more than this. We are faced here with the difficult question of how far faith consists in belief, how far it consists of other elements, and what those other elements are.

We can see something of the problem's difficulty from another, and even more famous, Christian text. In verse 13 of Chapter 13 of Saint Paul's first letter to the Corinthians he says, "In a word, there are three things that last forever: faith, hope, and love; but the greatest of them all is love." Faith, hope, and love (*caritas,* or charity, not *amor*) are the three theological virtues in Aquinas, who also says that formed faith is faith combined with charity: Hence it is possible to have faith (that is, unformed faith) that is not so combined.

Faith, it would seem, is something that a person may have without the other states to which in the Christian tradition it is thought to lead. But even though faith is distinct from them, it is not to be identified only with the cognitive or doxastic state of assent to the supposed truths of the tradition. Before passing judgment on the centrality of certainty in faith, we must look further at the other elements that faith has to include in addition to belief or knowledge. For the present I assume that belief or knowledge is essential and refer to it as the cognitive (or doxastic) core of faith. So far we have been considering the degree to which this cognitive core is under the control of the will. Let us now look at other factors with which it is combined.

There are a number of these, although it is not easy to separate them sharply from one another. The element most commonly stressed, especially by Protestant thinkers since Luther, is trust. The person who has faith does not merely believe certain things about God and his or her relationship to him but trusts God in consequence. This notion is not, in spite of the regularity with which it is mentioned without any analysis, a wholly clear one; but for the present we can say that if I trust God, that means that in consequence of the things I have come to believe about him, I am reassured about my future, about the world's future, and about there being a purpose and value in what happens to me and to the world. A result of that trust will be that I experience at least a lessening of the fears and anxiety that beset the human condition: fears of death and poverty, unease about the very presence of others and their intentions, discomfort in solitude, and the like.[7] Faith, then, includes or leads to a degree of serenity or at least a diminution of worry. We may describe this as the emotional or affective component in faith. A prominent feature of Jesus' preaching was his emphasis on the fact that his hearers, who supposedly knew that God cared for them more than the sparrows, nevertheless were not reassured by this knowledge but still allowed themselves to be harrowed by anxieties about their material needs and social status. They should have been serene in the face of their misfortunes but were not. This condition he explicitly describes in the New Testament as a failing in faith.[8] So far, then, we can discern trust and serenity as apparent elements in faith, in addition to its cognitive core, though each seems to be present there as a consequence of that cognitive core. Their nature and relationship, and in particular their relation to the will, need analysis.

Faith and Works

The problem of the relation of trust and serenity to faith has to be distinguished, at least prima facie, from the much-discussed problem of the relation of faith to works.[9] But here, too, the distinction is a hard one to make. In the writings of Paul and of Luther, we find great stress on the claim that what saves the Christian is faith rather than works. This claim seems to imply a sharp distinction, or even contrast, between them, which is apparently sharpened further when we recall that the works that are being distinguished from the faith that is said to save us are works that are undertaken for religious motives and are seen by those who perform them as commanded by God. But in spite of this distinction, there is no good ground to accuse either writer of indifference to works as the fruits of faith, though neither would accept that works without faith could lead to salvation.

There does seem to be a necessary connection between believing something and acting on it, though it is easy to state this connection too strongly. As Richard Swinburne says, "If I believe that it is more probable that this road leads to London than that that one does, and if my sole purpose is to go to London, necessarily I shall take this road rather than that road. In this way a man cannot but act on his beliefs."[10] The difficulty is to be clear about what it is to have a purpose and to extend the truth in this statement to cases where the belief does not seem to connect with any of our purposes. But the latter difficulty need not concern us here. For it is characteristic of religious beliefs that they come with purposes attached to them. It is manifestly incorrect to respond to a statement of the propositions that Jews, Christians, or Muslims believe by saying that they are true but merely interesting; for they are claims that demand a personal response and a change in life. To accept them as true, then, is to accept that the demands for change that they make should be among (indeed should be paramount among) our purposes. So a belief about the Jewish, Christian, or Islamic God is not in this respect like a belief about the right road to London; that belief is one I can have without wishing to go to London at all, so that its relation to my purposes can be stated wholly in subjunctives. A belief about God is a belief about a being who makes demands on the purposes I should have.

It is not possible here to analyze what it is to have a purpose. But we can say enough for the needs of our present argument. To have a purpose is to pursue, or to be strongly inclined to pursue, some objective. This is likely to be some objective that I want, though of course I can pursue an objective I do not want because doing this will help me gain some other objective I do want. I can, for example, choose to go to London even though I do not want to be there in order to attend a job interview or meet a friend. So if I come to believe in a God who demands that my purposes change, this is likely to involve me in coming to think that I have been pursuing some wrong objectives and neglecting some good ones through having the wrong wants or desires. If that is how I have been, however, I may have a personality that is dominated by wants that I now think I should not have and that lacks some desires that I now think I should feel. There is therefore a great obstacle to my pursuing those objectives that I have now come to believe I should seek after: I do not *want* to pursue them.

Does this show I do not have faith? It does rather obviously show that my faith is not very strong—which seems to imply that strong faith does issue in the actual pursuit of those purposes I believe (as part of its cognitive core) that I should be pursuing. So strong faith does lead to works. If someone has such faith, it will show. But this does not prove that if I am reluctant to get on with reforming my purposes, I have no faith at all. For although I may be reluctant, I may still realize, as I did not before, that I *should* change them. I suggest it is enough here that the believer have, at least weakly, what Frankfurt has called a second-order desire: a desire to have, or not to have, some other desire. The addict who is reforming will have a desire for a drug but will also have a desire not to have that desire; the sluggard forced into the school team may want to have the hitherto absent desire to score goals.[11] Presumably the devils Saint James speaks of, if they exist, lack even this second-order desire: They know God exists and wants them to have certain purposes, but they not only do not have them but also do not wish to have them. This is how Aquinas describes them, and he is therefore uncomfortable about conceding that they have faith at all. (He still seems to think they do, but this is implausible.[12]) It may indeed be possible for a person to accept that God exists but resent it; but to be said to have faith, someone must to some degree welcome it through accepting the need to have some of the purposes that he or she believes God requires.

Hence, although there is a connection in logic between faith and works, it is one that is compatible with faith's issuing in very few works indeed. Since belief in God is belief in a being who makes demands for change in us, acquiring such belief, if it is to help constitute faith rather than rejection, must prompt at least a desire to make those changes. This desire may well be weak, especially at first, and the changes may be hard to discern, especially from the outside. But it may instead be strong, and the first-order desires for wealth, power, and indulgence that God is thought to demand we change may be weakened at once; this is what happens in many of the more dramatic religious conversions.

Faith, however, is not the whole of religiousness, even in those traditions where it is most clearly thought essential. The works and deeds that are characteristic of the religious life, though they flow from faith, are not due to it alone. Saint Paul, for example, gives the palm among the fruits of grace, not to faith, but to love (*agape*). Aquinas says that faith without love (*caritas*) is unformed, though it is still faith. These classic statements suggest that, although love is supreme among those traits that the believer believes that he or she should have and is therefore, as it were, a target of faith, faith can be present without love following.

Love is commanded from the faithful. There are well-known puzzles about this, just as there are about belief. How can we be commanded to love? Can love be chosen? This is not the place to respond to these questions, but it is proper to say one thing that relates to our analysis of faith. If we look again at the preaching of Jesus, we find both a depiction of what love is and requires (namely, self-giving and forgiveness) and a reason his hearers should manifest it. The reason is that God treats them that way: He gives to them without regard to their merits. A natural human response is to say that we cannot reasonably be expected to treat others in this fashion because we, unlike God, have needs, fears, and anxieties that force us to protect ourselves from both natural hazards and other people. The core of Jesus' preaching of the Kingdom is that such self-protection is inconsistent with the recognition that God cares for each one of us and that the acknowledgment of his care for us will therefore *release* our capacity for love. Love (except for love of our own) is indeed too much to expect from us if we do not realize

God cares for us, but it becomes a possibility for those who do believe this. The desire for change in oneself meets the barrier of natural anxiety, but the barrier is one that a full recognition of the reality of God empowers us to surmount. In surmounting it, we achieve some of the serenity that releases our capacity for loving one another. Hence the full religious life is not supplied by faith alone, but faith is the necessary condition for its development. The link between faith and love is therefore the existence of trust. It is this concept that we must now examine.

Faith and Trust

Faith entails trust, not merely belief; it is *fiducia,* not merely *fides.*[13] Although often said, this statement needs exploration. What, in the first instance, is involved in trust? Is trust something that one feels or something that one does? Imagine a union representative entering some difficult negotiations and saying to fellow workers, "You must trust me to represent your interests adequately." Imagine a parent saying to a teenager while handing over the keys to the family car, "I will trust you to drive carefully." In both these cases trusting is something that one does. It is trust in this sense that Richard Swinburne defines when he says, "To trust a man is to act on the assumption that he will do for you what he knows that you want or need, when the evidence gives some reason for supposing he may not and where there may be bad consequences if the assumption is false."[14] The key word here is *act:* One chooses to guide one's actions toward the person in question by the assumption Swinburne describes. So trusting is here something one can clearly be said to do or not to do. It is also something that one can only do deliberately, in full knowledge that one is doing it. We may call trust of this sort explicit trust.

Explicit trust may very well increase tension and anxiety, not lessen them. It is hard to trust some people even when one knows one ought to; though if they keep their promises, represent us well, or drive carefully, trusting them gradually gets easier. What makes such deliberate trust hard is the evidence that the person we are trusting may very well not behave in these ways. So the firmness of our resolution to trust may in fact be something we summon in the face of doubts that we have about that person, and our resolution may not yield quietude until his or her actions subsequently justify it. When we are trusting someone (such as our own child) whom others have graver doubts about, our resolution may wear an obvious edge of bravado or self-consciousness that leads them to criticize us or smile indulgently.

But explicit trust is not the only kind. We can contrast it with the sort of trust that is characterized by the sheer absence of such doubts. This is the trust that children early in life have in their parents or that domestic animals sometimes seem to have in those who finally betray them by sending them to slaughter. This trust is also present in adult humans who unquestioningly accept what a dearly loved partner or family member tells them—until betrayal leads to disillusionment. The person trusting is here said to trust *implicitly,* a term that indicates both the totality of the attitude and the fact that it is innocently unformulated. One who trusts in this way may well have many other anxieties but none whatever concerning the role or intention of the person trusted, so that there is no reservation in dealing with that person and no disposition to protect oneself from that person. The goodwill and integrity of the person trusted are taken for granted. That such trust is unformulated may tempt us to suggest that the person trusting in this way does not have beliefs about the one trusted, but since it seems clear that one can have beliefs without being aware of having them, I am unmoved by this temptation.

Which sort of trust is present in faith? The answer is complex. If we turn once more to the preaching of Jesus, we find three things that bear directly on this question. The first, which we have already noted, is that he emphasizes that acceptance of the love of God should free believers from anxiety. The second is that he is frequently reported to have said that those healed by him owed their healing to their faith. The third is that he says entry into the kingdom of God is for those who are like children. Yet it is wholly impossible to read these teachings as implying that those who follow him are promised freedom from suffering, disease, or death.

I submit that we can infer the following answer to our question from these features of the Christian record. Implicit trust represents an ideal for faith in its unreservedness. But this unreservedness is the consequence of an innocence that faith in mature persons cannot have. For their faith is the result of explicit beliefs. When implicit trust is challenged by circumstances (such as betrayal), the trust may vanish or be lessened. If it is not, then it is probably replaced by explicit trust, that is, by trust that is maintained by moral resolution and is anxiety-laden on its own account. For the subject has come to realize that he or she has believed certain things about the other that may not be true. If trust persists after this, then it is inevitably of the explicit sort maintained by moral resolution.

I suggest that the teaching of Jesus implies that, although a wholly innocent trust is unavailable to mature persons, a full recognition of the nature of God nevertheless leads to a trust that is as unreserved as the implicit trust of the child: that the recognition of the full meaning of the belief in God that his hearers claimed to have is wholly liberating. But the fears and desires that the unregenerate life has implanted in those hearers ensure that their liberation is only partial. So they will need explicit trust; they will need to choose to behave in the ways that would be wholly and naturally forthcoming if such liberation were complete. To trust God explicitly rather than implicitly is to act in deliberate disregard of those fears and desires that would be absent if the anxieties that generated them were wholly removed by one's belief in him and to act instead from a second-order desire to weaken and ultimately to overcome them. The ideal of faith is the transformation of one's nature into a state of being where trust in God is wholly unreserved. The actual life of religious faith is a life spent with this ideal as a standard. This is not a life that the faithful expect to be free from suffering, but it is one in which they consider themselves, in varying degrees, to be safe in spite of it. An actual believer's life will involve a mixture of spontaneous and deliberate trust as well as frequent lapses into the fears and anxieties for which faith is believed to be an antidote.[15] These lapses require the counterbalance of the verbal and sacramental sustenance of communal religious life.

Trust, then, is, in part, a direct onset of serenity in consequence of belief in God and, in part, a deliberate policy of works and self-modification undertaken in consequence of that belief. Insofar as trust is the former, it is an affective response, and insofar as it is the latter, it is a conative response, to the supposed facts about God and his relation to ourselves that the believer has come to believe in.

The Need for Certainty

We can return now to the central question of this chapter: Is it necessary for faith to combine subjective certainty and objective uncertainty? I have already argued that objective uncertainty is not necessary. I now suggest that our brief discussion of the relation between the cognitive and noncognitive elements in faith shows that subjective certainty is not necessary either.

I leave for our next chapter the issue that is inevitably central for philosophical students of faith: its rationality or irrationality. I consider here only the question of whether the beliefs that form the cognitive core of faith need to be held with subjective certainty for the one who has them to be credited with having faith at all. (Although I have deferred the question of faith's rationality, I must say at once that if faith necessarily required subjective certainty, then in every case where this was not combined with objective certainty, defenders of faith's rationality would be hard put to make a case.) I suggest that the insistence that faith must involve subjective certainty, which is common to Aquinas and Kierkegaard, is due to an insufficiently clear distinction between ideal faith and actual faith (or faith as it is). I suggest further that this insistence is also due to an insufficient recognition of the relationship between the cognitive and noncognitive elements within faith.

When Aquinas tells us that faith is one of the supernatural virtues, he infers that the doctrine of the mean, which applies to all the natural virtues, does not apply to it. (We cannot have too much faith—or hope or love.) He similarly considers that faith is necessarily free of lapses, that is, of doubts. Whatever his motives, I suggest his inference is clearly mistaken if we look at actual faith. This seems to me to be similar to the natural virtues in that it can accommodate lapses in conviction, as the natural virtue of (say) courage can accommodate an occasional concession to fear or the virtue of temperance can accommodate an occasional self-indulgence. We do not judge someone to be without courage or temperance if he or she lapses in this way provided the lapse is uncharacteristic—provided, in other words, that it is indeed a lapse. Such lapses, paradoxically, even show that the one who is guilty of them has the virtue in question if he or she regrets them and tries to overcome them. Exceptions do prove rules sometimes. So it is with lapses in faith: The believer who has doubts does not show by this fact alone that he or she does not have faith; doubts that occur *within* faith are doubts that the believer tries to overcome, doubts with which he or she *contends*.

It is one of the many great merits of Richard Swinburne's analysis of faith that he argues, I think successfully, that one who has faith may well not hold the truth of his or her beliefs to be certain but merely to be more likely than those alternative cosmic schemes that he or she is in a position to consider seriously. It is vitally important to bear in mind that a rational being will respond with passion and determination to likelihoods (even low likelihoods) as well as to certainties. If I am informed there is a significant chance a loved one may not survive surgery, I will be naturally (and rationally) anxious; if I am informed there is a chance, even a slight one, that the plane's luggage contains a terrorist's bomb, I will be naturally (and rationally) inclined to suppress my impatience for takeoff and urge the authorities to check for as long as is necessary. In such cases we do not demand certainty as a condition for emotional involvement or determined decision.

It is surely the same with faith. Someone who is less than wholly certain of his or her beliefs, indeed is plagued with doubts about them, may nevertheless be so clear about their importance, and so impressed by the good that their truth would represent, that he or she is moved to disregard those doubts, show trust, and perform works that suggest (and may in time lead to) a greater degree of certainty. In such a faith deliberate and explicit, rather than instinctive and implicit, trust will have to dominate. But I submit that much faith is like this in practice and that the mere significant likelihood of the core beliefs of the faith being true (as distinct from a certainty that they are) may be enough to lead to some of the serenity that faith entails.[16]

A faith like this will have its own stresses. If unreserved trust in God is the ideal of faith, then doubts will be continual trials, and attempts to resolve them (rather than merely suppress them) will be sources of anxiety. There will be a constant ambivalence between viewing such doubts as lapses in trust (that is, as forms of personal disloyalty) and viewing them as counterevidence to the very being of God. These stresses will be added to those built into the religious life of even the most doubt-free believer, namely, those consequent on the fact that human nature is continually plagued with fears, desires, and anxieties that contend with the trust that all believers wish to show.

Kierkegaard likens faith to a passion and pours scorn on the suggestion that the life of faith could be based on judgments of probability. But the commitment of someone who responds to a saving message he or she thinks is merely likely to be true can be passionate and determined and may be manifested in the degree of concern such a person shows to resolve the doubts that such an epistemic situation inevitably allows to remain. To insist the commitment requires subjective certainty is to transfer that passion and determination from the believer's response to the cognitive core that prompts it, with gratuitously paradoxical consequences. Unless one is willing to deny the title of faith to the spiritual conditions of those who are like this, they demonstrate beyond reasonable question that subjective certainty, like objective uncertainty, is something that may indeed be present in faith but does not have to be. These considerations merely sharpen, for philosophers, the problem of how far, if at all, faith is a *rational* state. This problem occupies us next.

Notes

1. For a classic and bracing discussion of the concept of certainty, see "Certainty" in Moore 1959.

2. In the case of Aquinas, since he says that faith has "a more certain cause" (namely, God) than our convictions about lesser truths, it must be conceded that the belief that is the core of faith has more certainty in its object than other forms of assent. But it is still objectively uncertain in our present sense since the believer does not have either vision or conclusive grounds for assent. Compare *Summa Theologiae* 2,1 with IIaIIae 4,8.

3. Plantinga 1993b, 1993c.

4. I take Plantinga to have committed himself to rejecting the faith-knowledge dichotomy in arguing that believers may well have warrant for what they hold. See also Plantinga 1993a, 76.

5. IIaIIae 2,4 ad 2.

6. I quote here from the New English Bible, 1961.

7. It is not that I no longer think any of these things will happen but that I am not as anxious about them as I was.

8. Matthew 6:25–34.

9. I have commented on this issue before in Penelhum 1971b, Chapter 6.

10. Swinburne 1981, 27.

11. Frankfurt 1988, 11–25.

12. IIaIIae 5,2 ad 2.

13. I have dealt with this issue previously in Penelhum 1983, Chapter 8.

14. Swinburne 1981, 111.

15. To think one is safe in spite of sufferings, and to see fears and anxieties as mere lapses, is to be committed, in my view, to further beliefs about God and about one's own nature and future. I cannot explore this here, but see Penelhum 1979.

16. I suspect that this is the truth behind the occasional attempt—for example, that of Pojman—to say that faith can consist of hope. See Pojman 1986.

CHAPTER FIVE

Faith and Rationality

> *It is therefore quite certainly a great evil to have such doubts, but it is at least an indispensable obligation to seek when one does thus doubt; so the doubter who does not seek is at the same time very unhappy and very wrong. If in addition he feels a calm satisfaction, which he openly professes, and even regards as a reason for joy and vanity, I can find no terms to describe so extravagant a creature.*[1]

—Blaise Pascal

In this important but little-discussed fragment, Pascal attacks the attitude of those skeptics who find their inability to discern ultimate truths a source, not of distress, but of superiority and relaxation. He understands those who find doubt a source of anxiety; indeed, he sympathizes with them more than with those who enjoy an unconcerned certainty.[2] Those who doubt heedlessly, however, do not merely infuriate him but elicit this judgment: "This negligence in a matter where they themselves, their eternity, their all are at stake, fills me more with irritation than pity; it astounds and appalls me; it seems quite monstrous to me. I do not say this prompted by the pious zeal of spiritual devotion. I mean on the contrary that we ought to have this feeling from principles of human interest and self-esteem. For that we need only see what the least enlightened see."[3]

The Greek Skeptics were careful not to say that the limitations of reason provide rational grounds for an unperturbed mental state; Sextus said that *ataraxia* was something he found to follow by chance when one gave up the search for truth.[4] In spite of sharing the Skeptics' doubts about the powers of reason, Pascal maintains with passion that it is irrational to be complacently at ease when reason fails us. This has lessons for us when we consider how rational a state faith is.

Faith and the Modes of Rationality

When philosophers discuss faith and reason, they usually concern themselves exclusively with the epistemic status of the beliefs that the faithful have. What Pascal's diatribe against the complacency of skeptics shows us is that judging faith's rationality is more complicated. He is drawing our attention to a fact that many discussions of faith and reason overlook: The rationality of faith, or of its rejection, is not solely a matter of the certainty or probability of the propositions that the faithful believe and unbelievers do not believe. Judging the rationality of faith also involves assessing how those who have it and those who reject it respond to what they consider the status of these propositions. Pascal says that those who find themselves unable to decide whether these propositions are true ought, if they are rational people, to be distressed at this inability and to be overcome with humility rather than arrogance. If, like the Pyrrhonists, they consider that reason can never come to their rescue, then despair or anxiety is a more rational reaction than complacency. It is the essence of Pascal's apologetic to argue that the Pyrrhonists are right in this judgment, but "extravagant" to the point of insanity in their response to it.[5] It is not my purpose at this point to assess his apologetic or the Wager argument that forms part of it.[6] It is striking, however, that Hume, whose position on religion was as opposite to that of Pascal as anyone's could be, seems to have agreed with him on this and to have found skeptical arguments a path to gloom and anxiety, not release.[7] For all his search for equanimity, he did not see it as a simple consequence of recognizing that reason cannot answer ultimate questions for us. This is, on the contrary, something to which the resources of human nature have to reconcile us.

Ever since Aristotle, philosophers have recognized more than one sort of reason. They have recognized that we use our intellect to attain truth and also to guide our actions, and they have accordingly distinguished between theoretical and practical reason and between the virtues of theoretical and practical wisdom (or prudence). Arguments about the rationality of faith are usually about how far the beliefs at its core meet the debaters' standards for theoretical reason—whether these beliefs can be established by a priori or a posteriori reasoning and whether they are consistent with one another or are free of conceptual confusions. But we have already seen that assessing faith raises questions of practical reason, because we have to consider questions of doxastic obligation—about how prudent or how moral it is to form or sustain beliefs in this way or that. So even at the level of belief formation itself, issues of practical reason force themselves upon us, and we have to confront difficulties about how far the way we form our beliefs and the way we criticize them conform to standards that we think should govern our lives in other respects.

For the present I wish to note another important dimension of the rationality of human attitudes. Pascal says that insouciance is a transparently stupid reaction to the discovery of one's own ignorance. What he is drawing attention to here is the fact that we very commonly judge our emotions themselves in terms of their rationality. We say that someone's elation is foolish, that another's depression is in the cirumstances quite reasonable, or that a third person's indignation is justified. We judge emotions as being appropriate or inappropriate to the perceived facts and too strong or too weak in the light of those facts. It is reasonable to be moderately pleased if I win twenty dollars in a lottery but not reasonable to be transported with delight over it. It is quite appropriate to grieve if I think my lover has left me forever, but it is reprehensible to be delighted if my rival has been injured in a car accident. It is not possible to explore the details of this range of judgments here. But it is clear that common sense does not follow Stoicism in treating all emotions as intrinsically irrational or foolish, in spite of the deep influence of the Stoic opposition of reason and the passions. Nor does common sense follow Hume in supposing that a passion can be called unreasonable only if it is based on a false judgment ("and even then 'tis not the passion, properly speaking, which is unreasonable, but the judgment"[8]). Hume is mistaken. Not only is it reasonable to have quite strong emotions as a result of false judgments (as I might have if I am alarmed when I read a mistaken report in my hometown newspaper while on holiday that my house has burned down), but it also is unreasonable to have, or not to have, certain emotions as a consequence of judgments that are true (as I might when I am furious with the messenger who brings bad news or indifferent to the sufferings of my neighbors).

We can now apply these brief considerations to the rationality of religious faith. I have already argued that faith does not require that the beliefs at its core be held with certainty or that they fall short of knowledge. If these conclusions are sound, we can hazard the following. If I think it is certain, or even merely likely, that the proclamations of the faith are true, then it is surely rational for me to want to change in the ways the faith demands and to feel gratitude toward, and to repose trust in, the God who is the object of these proclamations. These responses will, as we have seen, be a mixture of affective responses and conative ones, of feelings and actions. But whichever of the two they are, they will be rational responses. Indeed, a tepid response along such lines is prima facie less rational than an enthusiastic or determined one, and the absence of enthusiasm or determination is likely to be ascribed by the believer to lingering moral weakness. We can add that even when the belief is an assent to the mere likelihood, rather than the assurance, of the proclamations' being true, a strong response may still be more rational than a weak one. Joy at a mere chance of forgiveness, or relief at the chance of avoidance of possible damnation, is far from an irrational attitude and is better than a casual or tepid response.

To say that these affective and conative responses are rational is to say that they are appropriate responses to the situation *as the believer perceives it*. It is, however, quite possible for someone who does not share the believer's perceptions of the situation to agree that the believer's responses are rational but still *mistaken*. And it is also true that the agreement that they are rational itself depends on an assumption that the beliefs on which they are based are not the result of gross violations of what the critic thinks to be our doxastic obligations. While Hume is wrong to think that a judgment of an emotion's rationality is wholly a consequence of the truth or falsity of the judgment that prompts it, it is still true that a negative evaluation of the way that judgment has been arrived at will often undermine the estimate of the rationality of the responses it causes. But even if we concede that those whose faith we are evaluating have based it on beliefs that do not violate doxastic obligations, we still judge their attitudes to be the *right* ones only if we think they are responding appropriately to the way things are, as distinct from the way they *think* they are. In other words, faith could well involve wholly rational attitudes and yet be mistaken.

It is impossible to overestimate the importance of this simple point. Even though philosophical critics of faith have often accused it of irrationality for inadequate and question-begging reasons, to concede its rationality is not to concede its truth. Nor does conceding that believers are rational in trying to change their lives in the ways their faith demands entail accepting that their attitudes and practices are the right ones. To accept that, one has to accept that there is at least a good likelihood that their beliefs are true.

As always, this has to be qualified! It is possible for someone who does not think the beliefs of a faith are true to nevertheless think that the way of life it teaches is good for the world. Although no longer a common view, it was found quite frequently in the first half of this century among those who had been brought up in a faith but had come to disbelieve. Some parents who no longer themselves believed thought it necessary to have their children taught the faith, perhaps as an anchor for their moral convictions. It is easy, yet mistaken, to ridicule this attitude. It is, after all, wholly possible to see a religion's vision of life and conduct as a desirable one while being unable to share its cosmic convictions and to decide (at least by implication) that the moral well-being of one's children dictates that some of their beliefs be inculcated for this reason rather than solely with an eye to metaphysical truth. This view of one's doxastic and pedagogical obligations is not patently absurd and is especially understandable in those who retain a nostalgia for a declining religiousness. Those who think this way do not think that the best attitudes are due only to true beliefs, although their practice shows that they *do* think that no one will *have* the right attitudes unless they acquire the beliefs to which they are the natural response.

This view of religion as false but desirable has all but vanished in our society, which is now more and more secularized. As religious beliefs have declined, the forms of personal transformation to which they give rise are increasingly thought to be quirky and even pathological. This leads to a moral and cultural standoff that is increasingly common and creates many stresses in a pluralistic world. This standoff comes about because, although the affective and conative changes that religion demands are rationally appropriate to the situation that the believer perceives, those who do not share that perception often find these changes life denying and destructive.

All the great religions of the world, theistic or not, tell us that we need personal transformation and that it is available to us if we follow the path of change that they proclaim. To convince us of this, they portray our present situation in terms that are far darker and gloomier than those that seem natural to common sense; for they are seeking to diagnose ills within us that we are reluctant to acknowledge but for which they think we need to seek a cure. They disagree about the nature of these ills: roughly, they divide into those who identify our key problems as moral and those who identify them as forms of ignorance. And they disagree accordingly on the nature of the cure that is required: Roughly, they divide between those who say we need moral transformation and those who say we need enlightenment. But whichever form of change a religion demands, it seeks to make that demand by convincing us of our plight. Hence for all the ultimate optimism of the world's great faiths, each depends for its initial impact on showing us that our present condition is worse than we think it is. This in turn involves negative criticism of the ways in which, at the individual and social level, we try to deal with the trials and limitations of that condition that we already recognize. What common sense considers reasonable forms of self-protection against risks, the faith has to interpret as self-deceiving attempts to conceal a deeper deficiency we do not wish to acknowledge. Those who reject the faith tend to see its demands and recommendations as antisocial hindrances that prevent the realistic attention to manageable problems in the interest of fanciful cosmic theories. They tend to see the faith's expectations for the future as facilely optimistic and utopian and as obstacles to the piecemeal measures of reformation and social engineering on which a more sober realism would dictate we should concentrate.

We therefore find increasing divergence in the estimation of the way of life that the faith requires and of its judgments of the unregenerate human condition. Recognizing that those who have faith are rational to follow the way that they proclaim does nothing to resolve this divergence; if anything, it worsens it. In particular, recognition cannot lessen the fact that believers and unbelievers will differ about what prudence dictates because they will differ about what is the good for human beings. (This difference is unaffected by the fact that they may agree readily enough about detailed matters of social policy.)

None of this is at all surprising, although it is often neglected. To expect those who believe in a moral and loving God and those who do not to have the same vision of human nature and its needs and capacities would be bizarre. This is not always borne in mind by those who debate how good or how bad religion is for us. If we bear it in mind as we should, it becomes obvious that the answers to such questions require a judgment about what our needs are. We may be unable to make such a judgment without first deciding whether the claims about those needs made by this or that religion are true or false.

Prudential Belief

We have seen that in judging the rationality of faith, we must consider more than the epistemic credentials of the beliefs that form its core and that when we recognize this, we can see that the ways in which those who have these beliefs respond to them can be judged as rational or irrational affections or as prudent or imprudent actions. This is an appropriate place to comment on a form of argument for faith that has achieved notoriety among philosophers: that the formation of the core beliefs themselves should be dictated or influenced by prudence. According to this argument, we should believe because it is in our interest to believe. We have seen that there can be doxastic policies; we must now consider the argument that prudent doxastic policy dictates the adoption of religious beliefs.

This argument appears in three places in the history of Western philosophical thought, which have been mentioned in Chapter 2. The most famous is in the fragment "Infini-rien" in Pascal's *Pensées;* the second, influenced by it, is in Butler's *The Analogy of Religion;* the third is in William James's philosophically slapdash but much-discussed essay "The Will to Believe."[9] Each is distinct and of great interest in its own right, but for present purposes I must take them together.

The prudential argument for religious belief is addressed to a supposed hearer who is genuinely doubtful about the truth of the faith's proclamations but thinks that at least there is some reasonable chance they might be true. The argument is emphatically not addressed to someone who has decided that they are certainly, or even probably, false. Pascal explicitly directs his Wager argument toward an imagined interlocutor who has adopted the Skeptic position that on the matter of the existence of God, reason can tell us nothing. Butler's argument targets an audience that was significant in his day, namely, the deists; they accepted on intellectual grounds that there is a God who designed the world but were doubtful whether the claims of revealed religion could be true. James has a particular thinker in his sights, namely, W. K. Clifford, who insisted that doxastic ethics required that one only adopt beliefs for which one has good evidence, although James openly uses Clifford as a representative of all those who give priority to the avoidance of error over the opportunity to seize on truth, at least in matters of religion.

These target audiences are not the same. What they share is a perception of epistemic uncertainty. Pascal is addressing a supposed hearer who has come, in Skeptic fashion, to think reason cannot decide whether there is a God (since, although there are signs that there is, there are also reasons to think there is not). James, in arguing in favor of religion and against Clifford's self-denying ordinance against faith, has to take for granted that the evidence in favor of religion is less than compelling. Butler is concerned to show those convinced that the God they believed in would not have revealed himself in the unclear and ambiguous ways the church says that they had come to accept his existence in the face of analogous counterevidence in nature. So he is trying to emphasize that his opponents were assuming a knowledge of God's nature and purposes that they had not assumed in becoming theists in the first place. Butler, then, is arguing that his audience needs to acknowledge its own ignorance, but he is at one with James in suggesting it should not be a barrier to the beliefs he is defending against them. In all three cases, the argument from prudence is mounted because the quality of the evidence or the demonstrations is judged to be inadequate by those who are resisting and is conceded to be inadequate by the apologist, for the sake of the discussion.

To the hearer in this position our three apologists urge that even though the truth may seem to be hidden in obscurity, it is supremely important that we not be mistaken about it. Butler expresses this view trenchantly: "The conclusion of all this evidently is, that, Christianity being supposed either true or credible, it is unspeakable irreverence, and really the most presumptuous rashness, to treat it as a light matter. It can never justly be esteemed of little consequence, till it be positively supposed false."[10] Only if we think that the claims of religion are false is it practically rational to treat them as unimportant. (There are, of course, some who have felt that the supposed falsity of religion makes it important to free believers from its shackles, but on the whole those who have rejected religion have not been as inclined to proselytize as those who have embraced it.) Here it is natural enough to suggest that if we do not think there is strong reason to accept the claims of religion, we may well not take as heated a view of their importance as Pascal and Butler do; surely it is only rational to treat as a matter of urgency those possibilities that seem likely ones. Is life not full enough of problems without those the prophets thunder about?

The answer of the prudential apologist is twofold; and, as we would expect, Pascal is the most clear and uncompromising. His response is in two parts. First, the content of the message of Christianity is that the price of making the wrong choice about the reality of God is the forfeiture of the eternal bliss that will be one's reward if the choice is right. So what is at stake here is nothing less than one's eternal destiny. Even if one is skeptical about the religion's message, the mere chance of its being true is enough to demonstrate the folly of not acceding to it. Second, it is no use saying that since one does not know what the truth is, it is better to hold off deciding; merely living forces that choice. We cannot not decide, for suspending decision is equivalent *in practice* to deciding that the claims of religion are false. His words are famous: "Oui, mais il faut parier. Cela n'est pas volontaire, vous êtes embarqués." (Yes, but you must wager. You have no choice, you are already committed.) William James's language is also well known here: The option that religion presents to us is momentous, and it is forced. The skeptical judgment may be epistemologically well based, but the skeptic's detachment is presumptuous rashness.

In these circumstances the prudential apologists all say that the prudent course is to gamble on the faith's being true. This raises another question: What does such gambling consist in exactly? Here Pascal and James are less ambiguous than Butler, who seems a little unclear whether he is merely recommending doubters never to give up on the study of the claims of Christianity or whether he wishes to follow Pascal in saying that they should try to bring about the belief in those claims that they do not yet have.[11] But his mentor here is in no doubt at all, and on this matter James, for all his lack of incisiveness in the rest of his essay, is in no doubt either: To gamble on God, one has to take steps to come to believe.

This is not all one has to do; or, more accurately, if one wants to do this, there are matters other than the belief itself on which one has to concentrate. The faith that it is prudent to acquire in view of the infinitely high stakes in the game of life demands more than mere assent; to gamble as prudence requires, one has to do one's best to meet these other demands. Pascal is clear that these demands are primarily those of piety: taking holy water, having masses said. Butler is also clear that a prudent person faced with the claims of Christian revelation would accede to what he calls the positive precepts of religion as well as the merely moral ones.[12] But although it is true that Pascal's argument is about gambling on God and not, at first sight, about *believing,* the satisfaction of the other demands of the faith is urged as a way to induce belief.[13] The hesitant doubter is urged to follow the example of others who have gone before and participate in the church's life of worship to dull his scruples, so that he will come to believe naturally. Belief is the product that will come as a result of doing those things that are its natural fruits in those who have it already.

Before assessing the prudential case for faith, let us be clear about what it proposes. It recommends to a doubter that he or she should adopt the way of life of the faith in the hope that faith itself will replace doubt; and it recommends that this be done because of the transcendent importance of not choosing wrongly in a cosmic game in which each of us, by the sheer fact of being alive, is involved. It does not suppose that the steps it recommends as a means of acquiring faith themselves constitute faith. Pascal clearly thinks that real faith is a gift of divine grace and recommends the regular performance of religious duties as a way of dulling the influence of those human passions that obstruct our receptiveness to faith. So it would be foolish to dismiss what he says on the ground that no state of mind controlled by self-interest can be real faith. Pascal never supposes that it could be; he only points out that by rejecting faith, one may well be throwing away one's salvation. If we follow his recommendations, we may end up having the real thing. Following those recommendations is not the real thing. He says as much in another fragment, in case we have missed it: "Custom is our nature. Anyone who grows accustomed to faith believes it, and can no longer help fearing hell, and believes nothing else."[14]

How are we to judge the prudential argument for faith, thus understood? I suggest that, although there are serious difficulties in it, they are not the ones that come most readily to mind or the ones that are most commonly offered. The argument is often thought to be morally objectionable either because it urges faith in an unworthy manner or because it tries to persuade us to ride roughshod over our doxastic obligations.[15] I think we have already seen that objections of this sort miss the point. A prudential awareness of the fact that salvation may have conditions is something to be found in the paradigms of preaching.[16] Nor can a deep and intense concern with the reader's spiritual needs be missed by any serious student of Pascal or Butler. But the impotence of these objections is best seen from the fact that the prudential apologist is not supposing that the course he recommends is itself the life of faith; it is merely a path toward faith for someone who is open to persuasion that faith would be a prudentially wise thing to have. Such an argument does not commit its user, or its hearer, to the view that someone who has come to have it is *then* motivated by prudence—for anyone still so motivated has not yet acquired faith. I know of no theological argument worth consideration that could show that someone who seeks to acquire it on prudential grounds would be barred by God from coming to have it. Furthermore, the argument assumes that the hearer does not think that the consideration of evidence, or the use of philosophical argument or any other form of the exercise of theoretical reason, can show whether the faith is true. Theoretical considerations are ruled out before the argument begins. However we analyze the nature of wishful thinking or self-deception, we must recognize that each involves a potentially culpable inattention to evidence and argument; the prudential argument for faith presupposes that its hearer has come to despair of these as sources of truth but can see that true belief about the matters of faith might be of the last importance. In such a situation prudential considerations do not run counter to our doxastic duty to seek truth; they are the only rational considerations left to us when our intellects have failed to find it.

These things are enough to show that for those who are in the condition it presupposes, the prudential argument for faith is a serious and wholly proper one. But it still runs into lesser but nevertheless real difficulties. In the first place, how is one to be sure that one has indeed exhausted the possibilities of an intellectual determination of the truth? For example, how many alternatives to the faith does one have to consider before deciding this? If one is confronted by four or five or twenty-five cosmic schemes, and two or three seem slightly more likely than the others but about equal to one another on the scales of probability, is that a situation where reason can be judged to have reached its limit? If so, exactly why? Questions like these are extraordinarily hard to answer and even to formulate in appropriate ways.

James tries to address them in a way that neither Pascal nor Butler does, with his famous but obscure distinction between live and dead options. For many Westerners, for example, the options between Confucianism and Taoism, or between Theravada and Mahayana Buddhism, are not the live ones they are to Chinese, Japanese, or Tibetan inquirers. Although clear enough on the surface, this distinction merely seems to mean that there are many possible worldviews that such inquirers have not had the opportunity, or taken the trouble, to study. Nevertheless, a rational individual may well feel that he or she can go on weighing the pros and cons of this faith or that indefinitely, yet the passage of time and the other pressures of life demand a decision—a fact James encapsulates in his rather clearer concept of a forced option. So the prudential argument presupposes a prior elimination of many alternatives and a finite range of choices among which the hearer is choosing without any perceived reason for preference other than prudential ones; but when this set of conditions is satisfied is not going to be easy to say.

Given that someone may well *feel* that he or she satisfies this condition without being able to specify why, we must next notice that there are certainly problems of detail about the practical prescriptions that the prudential apologist offers. There is a problem about whether they will work, and there is a problem about how far someone who does not have faith already can satisfy them. On the first of these Pascal is the most forthcoming. There seems little doubt that he would think that faith is a divine gift and that no one, including himself, can predict that the search for it will succeed.[17] But it is clear from the fragment previously quoted that Pascal thinks also that the *habit* of religious observance will have the effect of dulling the passions that he sees as primary obstacles to faith. The Wager fragment concludes with his telling the interlocutor that others have preceded him in acting as if they already believed and that they have come to have real belief in consequence. It is clear also that many who have faith but are assailed by doubts are sustained through them by the continued performance of religious duties and that this experience within faith is being extrapolated, rightly or wrongly, to the cases of those who do not have it yet but want to.

The second difficulty is more serious. The life of religious faith demands that one perform actions that include duties toward God as well as duties toward other human persons. In Butler's language, religion enjoins positive precepts as well as moral ones. These include duties of worship, prayer, and sacramental participation. (Pascal mentions masses and holy water.) Neither Pascal nor Butler seems to recognize (and the point is equally alien to James) that at least some of these are actions that an unbeliever may well be unable to do. An unbeliever can kneel and speak and eat and drink, but these are only the outward part of these actions. Consider the following passage from the Thirty-Nine Articles of the Anglican church: "The Sacraments were not ordained of Christ to be gazed upon, or to be carried about, but that we should duly use them. And in such only as worthily receive the same they have a wholesome effect or operation: but they that receive them unworthily purchase to themselves damnation, as Saint Paul saith."[18]

At least some of the duties whose performance the prudential apologist recommends as routes toward the acquisition of faith cannot, it seems, be performed unless one already has it. Butler, for example, who tells us that religion "consists in submission and resignation to the divine will,"[19] nevertheless seems to see no difficulty in recommending the serious but unconvinced inquirer to exercise prudence by acting as if Christianity were true; yet an inner acknowledgment that what one is doing is in fact the will of God seems to be of the essence of at least some of the duties that Christians undertake. In briefer terms, it does not seem possible to recommend that *worship* be undertaken purely from prudential considerations since worship includes inner as well as outer actions, and the inner actions include or entail the very belief that is here supposed to be still in the future.

There is a third difficulty. Many have difficulty conceding that it would be just for creatures to be deprived of eternal happiness (let alone be subjected to eternal suffering) for not believing. This difficulty is only slightly eased if one agrees that believing is indirectly under our control and that we do indeed have doxastic obligations. The difficulty is not much softened if one goes further and agrees with the superficially implausible view that anyone who conscientiously tries to discharge those obligations and is free of self-deception must come to accept the faith—in other words, that unbelief is always morally blameworthy or sinful. For even if both are true, such a penalty still seems to some too great to be a just return for such offenses.

If we feel this (the problem does not arise if we do not), then following the recommendation of the prudential theist would involve us in worshiping a deity whose cosmic policies seemed to us to be immoral. Worship, once more, involves more than outward form; it involves admiring and approving what the God who is worshiped does. I can only pretend to worship a being with whom I morally disagree. So it is not clear that the inquirer who feels this way can follow the program that the prudential apologist sets out. But even if the inquirer can, the program has as its objective a faith that involves a positive judgment about a cosmic policy that the inquirer does not consider moral before the program begins; and this is no longer a program to instill belief where reason can tell us nothing but a program to change a belief on which reason has already pronounced.[20]

It is only cosmic schemes that require belief for salvation that provide a ground for supposing that prudence requires religious belief when the independent grounds for it are inadequate. Those that do not may well appeal more strongly to the undecided on moral grounds, but the prudential arguments for adopting them are inevitably weaker. These are only some of the perplexities that beset prudential apologetics. They seem to me to be the most serious. In spite of them, I suggest that the case for prudential apologetics has considerable strength in a religiously ambiguous world.[21] It does not merit the hasty dismissal that it commonly provokes.

The Basic Belief Apologetic

The rationality of faith is not only a matter of the epistemological status of the beliefs that are its core. But this matter has always been the center of consideration for philosophers. We have seen that in modern times a decision on the rationality of faith has commonly been supposed to depend on the success or failure of natural theology. We have also seen that this supposition has been due to the foundationalist objectives of epistemology since Descartes, although the belief in the apologetic importance of natural theology, like natural theology itself, predates these objectives and so cannot depend entirely upon them.

I cannot comment directly here on the common opinion that natural theology cannot succeed. I have discussed it elsewhere and merely say here that even if it has so far failed, this does not prove it must always do so.[22] Showing that it must fail requires demonstrating claims about the limits of our intellectual capacities that are at least as controversial as the arguments of natural theology themselves. I am concerned here with the question of how far the rationality of faith depends on the possibility of any natural theologian succeeding.

The natural theologian seeks to prove some key religious propositions or to show at least that they are probably true. What makes such a thinker a *natural* theologian is the fact that his or her arguments begin from premises that are not themselves religious propositions: propositions that we can know to be true without knowing that God exists, for example. The knowledge of religious truths that would come through natural theology, then, would be mediate or inferred knowledge. If it is true that the rationality of religious beliefs depends on the possibility of natural theology succeeding, then it follows that the rationality of faith depends on the existence, or at least the possibility, of mediate or inferred knowledge of religious truths. This has been vigorously contested by some contemporary apologists, and it is their arguments against it that I wish to examine now.

Natural theology is still practiced. There have been striking twentieth-century attempts to revive the Ontological Proof, the Cosmological Proof, and the Design Argument. The most systematic and impressive work in natural theology is generally agreed to be that of Richard Swinburne.[23] These attempts have to some extent been upstaged, however, by arguments intended to show that sucess in natural theology is not necessary. Some of those who argue in this way do not think success in natural theology is impossible; indeed, they include philosophers (such as Alvin Plantinga) who have practiced it. But they argue nevertheless that we should reject the assumption common to many of its practitioners and its critics that if natural theology is impossible, religious belief lacks rational justification. They urge that religious belief is, or at least can be, rational and justified without this.

Their fundamental claim is that religious beliefs can be rational without being held through inference from other beliefs. They can be both rational and *basic.* In Plantinga's language, religious beliefs can be *properly basic* beliefs. I call this defense of belief in God the Basic Belief Apologetic. It is also known as Reformed Epistemology in view of its likeness to what Plantinga claims is the underlying position of the sixteenth-century Reformers, particularly Calvin.[24] The best-known proponents of this apologetic position are William Alston, Alvin Plantinga, and Nicholas Wolterstorff.[25] Even though the demands of brevity make it necessary for me to consider their work together here, I attempt to avoid the error of confusing one thinker with another.

I begin with the negative arguments found against the demand for independent justification for religious beliefs. This demand is attributed to the influence of what is called classical or Enlightenment foundationalism, and it is commonly dubbed "evidentialism."[26] The attack on this demand has taken two allied forms. The first, found clearly in essays by Plantinga, emphasizes that it is not possible to state the epistemological requirements of classical foundationalism in a form that does not itself violate them. The second emphasizes that a demand for independent justification of religious beliefs imposes a condition of rationality on them that we do not impose in practice on the beliefs of secular common sense. This latter emphasis gives the Basic Belief Apologetic an important resemblance to the apologetic of skeptical fideism. It is important, however, to be clear how far this resemblance extends and where it ceases.

Plantinga first attacks classical foundationalism as being internally incoherent. When the classical foundationalist maintains that it is rational to hold a belief only if that belief is a self-evident truth, is about an unquestionable appearance of sense, is otherwise incorrigible, or is a belief that one can infer from a truth of one of these kinds, then this claim itself must be in one of these classes. But there is no reason to suppose that this claim is and good reason to think that it is not; "it is no more than a bit of intellectual imperialism on the part of the foundationalist."[27] Although classical foundationalism may be right that self-evident and incorrigible propositions are properly basic, to say this is not to state something that is itself self-evident or incorrigible; to do so merely represents an unargued commitment of the epistemologist who holds it. It does not in any way provide support for the view that there cannot also be other classes of belief that are properly basic. For all we know, these may include belief in God.

This argument seems unanswerable, but (like other self-referential refutations in philosophy) it leaves a deep unease. It is this unease to which a great deal of Plantinga's subsequent work in epistemology has been directed and to which Alston also responds. Modern foundationalism may well show us no formally acceptable reason that belief in God should not be held without being inferred from beliefs of other kinds, but it is easy enough to think of reasons we might suppose this. If we put aside any requirement of independent justification, we seem to open the way to anybody's dogmatic assertions and to a potential chaos of clashing convictions. For if one does not need *reasons* for one's religious assertions, surely one enthusiast's leap of faith is as good as anyone else's? As Locke expressed the matter, not so long after the Thirty Years' War, in which so many of the faithful had been busy slaughtering each other, "every conceit that thoroughly warms our fancies must pass for an inspiration, if there be nothing but the strength of our persuasions whereby to judge of our persuasions."[28]

This concern urgently demands an answer, and much of the development of the Basic Belief Apologetic since the appearance of Plantinga's first two or three essays propounding it can be seen as a series of attempts to provide this answer. I think these attempts are reasonably successful, but the success is bought at the price of revealing that the apologetic has important limitations.

For the moment I continue with Plantinga's argument. He emphasizes that, although a believer may hold his or her belief in God without inferring it from other beliefs (that is, as a basic belief), it does not follow that such belief in God is groundless. A belief can be grounded (and therefore be potentially rational) without being based on evidence or otherwise inferred from beliefs of other kinds. Plantinga proceeds to draw an analogy between belief in God and other, secular beliefs that are also held without being inferred but that we have no temptation (unless we are epistemological skeptics) to declare groundless or arbitrary. This analogy between religious and secular beliefs is prominent in the trilogy of which, at the time of this book, he has published the first two volumes and is central to the similar argument for the rationality of Christian belief developed by William Alston in *Perceiving God.*

Since Descartes, epistemologists who have tried to offer refutations of skepticism have tried repeatedly to argue that we have sufficient reasons for treating our sense experiences as reliable guides to the nature of the physical world "outside" us. Some have also tried to fend off skeptical doubts about memory, induction, or beliefs about the mental lives of other people. One of the most important elements in the tradition of skeptical fideism is what I have elsewhere called the Parity Argument. This tells us that the repeated failure of such attempts shows that the skeptical tradition is right to question the possibility of providing reasons for our commonsense convictions in these matters. The Parity Argument also tells us that we should recognize that the absence of good independent reasons for belief in God should not make us hesitate to accept his existence any more than the absence of philosophical guarantees of commonsense convictions makes us hesitate to use our eyes, ears, memory, and powers of inductive thinking to form beliefs about our daily world. This point is sometimes expressed in popular sermonizing by the claim that daily secular living and even science require faith as much as religion does.

The Basic Belief Apologetic is, at least verbally, different from this. It does indeed in all its forms stress analogies between belief in God and sensory, inductive, or memory beliefs. But just as its practitioners do not say that all arguments of natural theology fail, so they do not say, with the skeptic, that our commonsense beliefs are outside the scope of reason. These apologists are rather concerned to suggest that the criteria of rationality that foundationalist thinkers since Descartes have assumed are too narrow.

I cannot enter here into such questions as the justification of induction or the reliability of sense perception. It is enough to notice that the Basic Belief Apologetic emphasizes that belief in God that is not inferred from privileged nontheistic premises is not, on that account alone, to be dismissed as irrational, unless we are also prepared to dismiss as irrational a whole mass of beliefs of other kinds that we also acquire as basic beliefs. The appeal to parity is essential to this argument, but the skeptical denial of the rationality of uninferred beliefs is not.

What is it that preserves the rationality of properly basic beliefs? What prevents them from being "groundless"? It seems to be that they arise from *experiences* of certain sorts. It is very important to see that when we have these characteristic experiences, they do not function as premises from which we infer the beliefs they occasion. Rather, the beliefs are occasioned (or "called forth") by them. It is not that I first know that I have certain auditory whining experiences, and certain doggy visual experiences, and that from this fact about my stream of consciousness I then infer that my dog wants to go out for a walk. Rather, when I have these experiences, they occasion, or trigger, the belief that he does.

In post-Cartesian epistemology attempts to show that we are entitled to believe things about the "external world" on the basis of sense experience have always foundered because of their circularity. Just as Descartes himself is commonly accused of arguing in a circle when he uses his reasoning powers to prove the reality of the God who guarantees that his reason will not deceive him, so those who follow Descartes in attempting to proceed from starting points in human consciousness to conclusions about the world beyond it regularly find themselves justifying this by reference to facts about that world that such an argument is designed to show we can know. To say that our senses are reliable, for example, on the grounds that if we make predictions on the basis of sensory experiences obtained in standard circumstances, we are likely to predict successfully, is to assume we know that there is a plurality of perceivers, that they can distinguish standard from aberrant circumstances, and that they have had success when they have made predictions on this basis. Where else but through sensory observation could we come to know these things? This does not show that these considerations are valueless in understanding the ways in which we learn about our world through the senses, but it does show that if we begin from a generalized skepticism about the senses' reliability, there is no philosophical escape from it.

In the forms of belief formation used as analogies in the Basic Belief Apologetic, therefore, we have a characteristic phenomenology

that accompanies the formation of these beliefs. It is this, in conjunction perhaps with other circumstances, that preserves our most
common and fundamental doxastic practices from groundlessness.
In the case of sense perception, the phenomenology consists in our
being "appeared to" in various ways: visually, auditorily, and so on.
In the case of memory beliefs, there are characteristic representa-
tional phenomena within consciousness that accompany recollec-
tion.

The analogy with sense perception is central to the defense of religious belief formation developed by Alston in *Perceiving God.*
Alston argues that epistemological defenses of sense perception
against skepticism cannot be stated in ways that escape circularity
but that our doxastic practice of forming beliefs about the world
through perception is justified through being socially established
and through containing tests for distinguishing between well-
founded and ill-founded sensory beliefs. It is not possible here to
debate his claim that the rationality of our participation in a doxastic practice is not undermined by the circularity of attempts to justify it. It is enough to agree that if this claim fails, the alternative is
indeed some sort of skepticism about that doxastic practice. Alston
then points out that if the claim is accepted, a parallel claim about
the doxastic practice of basing Christian beliefs on supposed direct
experience of God (which he calls Christian Mystical Practice) can
be dismissed as irrational only if we apply a double standard. For
Christian Mystical Practice is also socially established and contains
within it ways of distinguishing between well-founded and ill-
founded religious claims.

The strength of this argument, which is considerable, depends
critically on the existence of phenomenological counterparts in religion of the appearances of sense and on a demonstration that the
obvious *differences* between Christian Mystical Practice and the
formation of beliefs through sense perception do not undermine
the status of the former as a viable and autonomous mode of belief
formation. The most obvious disanalogy is the fact that, whereas
the latter practice is universal, the former is not. I think that on
both counts the argument is successful. Believers who think they
have encountered God directly have indeed had experiences that it
is reasonable for them to interpret as appearances or perceptions of
God. That only some people have such experiences has, within the
standards of Christian Mystical Practice, explanations that would

lead one to expect them to be available only to some. We have already encountered these in our earlier discussions of the obstacles to acceptance of religious beliefs: For example, such beliefs look too personally demanding for some of us, so we may well close our minds to the possibility of the sorts of experience that could generate beliefs of this kind.[29]

What all this shows, if it is true, is that it is reasonable for those who engage in Christian Mystical Practice to do so. But this only provides what Alston calls prima facie justification. The very fact that any doxastic practice has to include within it ways of deciding when a particular belief is acceptable and when it is not shows that such a practice may turn out to yield false beliefs on some occasions or even on every occasion. Rational beliefs can, after all, be false.

Before proceeding further, I wish to comment on Plantinga's recent development of his version of the Basic Belief Apologetic in the first two volumes of his ongoing trilogy in religious epistemology. His earlier essays began by pointing out the arbitrariness of the evidentialism of the classical foundationalist critique of religion and continued by stressing that belief in God could be basic (that is, noninferred) but still not lack grounds. For it might have a characteristic phenomenology and be held in circumstances that justified it. In his most recent writing Plantinga makes a distinction between two aspects of the rationality of beliefs: justification and warrant. A belief is justified if those who have it have come by it in ways that fulfill their doxastic obligations: They have not neglected to look or listen or read and have not been bigoted or biased. But one can fulfill all such conditions but still not have warrant for what one believes. Warrant is that "elusive quality or quantity enough of which, together with truth and belief, is sufficient for knowledge."[30] I can perform all my doxastic duties conscientiously but still have bad luck and believe falsely or believe truly merely by accident. The religious believer is not lacking in justification for his or her beliefs merely because they do not conform to the standards of the classical foundationalist; but this merely shows that the believer has not violated any doxastic obligations by not adhering to those standards. But there is more to be said in response to those who think that religious beliefs that do not conform to those standards are groundless. They are not merely not groundless but may well constitute knowledge if they have warrant. A believer has warrant for a true belief if the belief, in addition to being true, is the product of some cognitive faculty or mechanism that is functioning as it should in its proper environment and is aimed at truth.

This complex analysis of warrant is spelled out in *Warrant and Proper Function* and is developed in contrast to other epistemologies, which are criticized, in *Warrant: The Current Debate*. Plantinga accepts from "reliabilist" theories of knowledge that we may well know things without having privileged access to the nature of the processes that yield our knowledge. For example, we may well know many things through perception or memory without understanding how this comes about, provided we have reliable sensory or memory faculties. Our faculties have to be functioning in a way that is up to standard, however, and in settings for which they are designed. And they have to be faculties whose aim is truth. For it is possible that some belief-generating mechanisms are aimed, not at truth, but at survival or comfort or happiness. This is the case, for instance, in the clearly unwarranted conviction of patients with life-threatening diseases that they will recover; such a belief is probably the product of the proper functioning of a belief-generating mechanism that aims at survival, not truth.[31] If this complex of conditions is satisfied, a true belief is warranted.

The key to this epistemology is that there are many such mechanisms that generate warranted beliefs, not just the mechanisms that generate the sorts of belief that satisfy the demands of classical foundationalism. This last point is due historically to Reid. The strength of his "Common Sense" epistemology consists in large measure in recognizing the dogmatic and arbitrary character of the fundamental criteria of rational belief that we find in post-Cartesian theory of knowledge, particularly (or so he says) in Hume. Reid maintains we are constituted in such a way that each of us has a repertoire of basic beliefs that cannot be justified by philosophy without circularity but that can only be exposed to the tender mercies of skepticism by selecting some as paradigms and rejecting others because they are different. Plantinga, following him, argues that our repertoire includes beliefs about ourselves, memory beliefs, beliefs about other persons, beliefs due to testimony, a priori beliefs, perceptual beliefs, and inductively formed beliefs, and he promises to complete the impressive argument of his trilogy by showing that theistic beliefs form part of this repertoire also.[32]

The Basic Belief Apologetic, of which the foregoing is only the sketchiest summary, has rightly been very influential. It has freed philosophical defenses of religious belief from the restrictions of a tradition in the theory of knowledge that has likely run its course. The apologetic forces us to take a new look at the assumption that beliefs need evidence before they are rationally justifiable. And it is at least not crassly fideistic in that it neither requires the denial of the value (as opposed to the necessity) of independent intellectual support for religious beliefs nor denies that many of them can be so inferred. It also recognizes that both basic and inferred religious beliefs, like basic and inferred beliefs of other sorts, are subject to what Alston calls "overriders" and Plantinga (after John Pollock) calls "defeaters": They are subject to correction by other experiences or by reasoning. There is no claim to infallibility lurking in the wings. Nor is the frequent appeal to religious experience the same as the classical "Argument from Religious Experience"; that argument was a minor form of traditional natural theology that sought to infer the truth of theistic beliefs from the fact that some people have experiences that seem to them to be encounters with God. The Basic Belief Apologetic argues that there is no good reason to reject the claim that many people do in fact perceive or encounter him and that this is the source of their basic beliefs. A critic who says at this point that this argument assumes the truth of the very beliefs it is defending can indeed be accused of an epistemic double standard.

I wish now to explore the reasons this apologetic still generates unease. There is, in the first place, some uncertainty about how important the analogy between religious beliefs and commonsense secular beliefs (especially perceptual beliefs) is. In Alston's apologetic it is clearly central since he sees himself as showing that Christian Mystical Practice (in which, as he sees the matter, participants have direct experience of God) is a doxastic practice in which we are justified in having confidence, and he directs many of his arguments to showing that the differences between it and sense perception are to be expected and do not give reason to undermine that confidence. This narrows the primary apologetic attention to those religious experiences that generate and reinforce beliefs about God through supposed encounters with him. Such occasions manifest what Alston calls "mediated immediacy":[33] a state of consciousness in which one is aware of a reality that appears directly but in which the state of consciousness itself can be distinguished from that reality. Ordinary perceptual consciousness fits this model, and so does direct experience of God, even though this may well have no *sensory* content. Alston takes great care to provide at least a framework for discussing the phenomenology of such experiences, and he also devotes much of the later argument of the book to examining the relationship of such experiences to other supports of religious belief, such as testimony and authority. I think we must recognize that many believers, while conceding their relative spiritual poverty in comparison with the great prophets or mystics of their faith, do not claim such direct encounters for themselves or at least think of them as rare in their own lives. It is important for any apologetic that centers on such experience to show how those who believe with little or none of it justify their acceptance of the authority of those major formative figures to whom they would point as sources of their own conviction.

If, however, we consider some of the examples Plantinga offers as grounds or occasions for beliefs about God, it is less clear that the existence of a distinctive phenomenology is central to his argument.[34] He says that on reading the Bible, "one may be impressed with a deep sense that God is speaking to him," or one may feel guilty at some wrongdoing and form the belief that God disapproves of one's act or feel after repentance that one has been forgiven by God. It is possible, but not at all compelling, to interpret these occasions as having a distinctive religious phenomenology—except, of course, the awareness of the onset of the very convictions whose status such occasions are being used to support. I refer to those occasions when some event that is otherwise phenomenologically unremarkable religiously occasions a religious conviction that the subject has not had before as "intimations." At least some of Plantinga's examples are intimations in this sense. If we call such occasions examples of religious experience, we must bear in mind that there is nothing present in them phenomenologically that would not also be present in the experience of someone who failed to form the conviction in question in what would otherwise be the same set of circumstances.

It is interesting to note here that in *Warrant and Proper Function*, where Plantinga follows Reid in stressing the wide variety of properly basic beliefs that we form at the secular level, he notes a special phenomenology in some cases but does not note one (because there is none) in others. There is a special phenomenology for sense perception, for memory, and for some a priori beliefs, but none is discernible for inductive beliefs or beliefs based on testimony. Here there seems merely to be a belief-forming mechanism but no distinctive type of experience that is relevant to their epistemic status. If what is key to the analogy between secular and religious beliefs is that each is grounded in a belief-forming mechanism that has an attached system of overriders or defeaters, then the presence of a distinct phenomenology does not seem to be as important; nor, if there is such a phenomenology, does it have to be one that lends itself readily to the language of "appearing."[35]

But if the analogy with established secular beliefs does not depend on the presence of a distinct religious phenomenology, do we not find ourselves back with situations in which believers do the very thing that Locke was afraid enthusiasts do and offer us nothing but the strength of their persuasions whereby to judge of those persuasions? Why should I be persuaded of the epistemic validity of the experience of another when it consists merely of his being persuaded? For that matter, ought I to pay attention to such events when they occur in my own stream of consciousness? Or should I suspect them?

This reaction may well seem to some to be a mere reassertion of the basic dogma of classical foundationalism. Let us examine this. If we put aside the skeptic and see the task of the apologist as that of bridging the divide between believers and doubters who already share a wide range of secular commonsense convictions, then the presence or absence of a distinctive religious phenomenology can assume a real significance. For that phenomenology can be used to reinforce the analogy between religious experiences and the practice to which they are central and those secular doxastic practices (most obviously sense perception) where there also is a distinctive phenomenology. If doubters do not have those experiences, that (epistemically speaking) is their loss; and regardless of whether they do, they have the special duty of explaining them away. The burden of the argument lies with the doubters. If, however, religious experience does not include a distinctive phenomenology, and the apologetic that centers on it offers us merely a doxastic machinery that generates convictions, then (even though there are secular commonsense doxastic machineries, such as indictive thinking, that do this also and do it without a distinctive phenomenology) doubters can simply say that the religious machinery is absent, or does not work, for them. In responding in this way, they are doing nothing inconsistent with their prior acceptance of secular commonsense convictions. We all know that there are doxastic mechanisms that work for some and not for others (such as those that generate belief in homeopathy or astrology, to take two moderately controversial examples at opposite ends of the spectrum of educated opinion). This does not, it hardly needs to be said, constitute any sort of refutation of the believer's doxastic practice; here Plantinga is wholly and importantly right. But it does show that there is nothing in the doubters' refusal to endorse that doxastic apparatus that represents a violation of *the doubters'* doxastic obligations.[36] Plantinga's argument here is a successful negative (or defensive) apologetic, not a positive one.[37]

I want to put this point in terms of Plantinga's language of warrant. Plantinga explains warrant as something that only true beliefs have. It looks on the surface as though a false belief could have it: If warrant is that which, if added to true beliefs, yields knowledge, then whatever fulfills this role might well be something that could be added to false beliefs too, even though it could not yield knowledge in their case. But Plantinga defines warrant in detail as something we have when a doxastic mechanism functions as it should and is aimed at truth. So to ascribe warrant, thus described, to religious beliefs is to presuppose there *is* religious truth. The believer is indeed in violation of no doxastic obligation in presupposing this; but the doubter is in violation of none by declining to. So it seems, at least, if there are no distinctive phenomenological features of the relevant religious experiences that would do something to reinforce the claim that the doxastic mechanisms of which they are a part are aimed at truth, as distinct from comfort, survival, or some other value.

I suggest, therefore, that any version of the Basic Belief Apologetic that does not center on those forms of religious experience that have a distinctive phenomenology that parallels that of sense perception will, even in a postfoundationalist context, serve only as a negative, and not as a positive, apologetic. It must now be said that, although a version, like Alston's, that does center on this parallel is for that reason far stronger, it has to contend (as Alston recognizes) with naturalistic attempts to explain such experience away. I think such naturalistic explanations are as strained in many cases as he thinks they are, however. I therefore conclude that as things now stand in contemporary debates about religious epistemology, the Basic Belief Apologetic is a successful form of negative apologetics, and insofar as it centers on the phenomenologically distinctive features of what Alston calls Christian Mystical Practice, it offers a form of positive apologetic that it is for the naturalistic critic of faith to answer. But I must qualify this statement at once. For it is obvious that a parallel case could be made for other forms of faith than the one Alston is concerned to defend. In exploring the implications of this, we have to contend with the pervasive phenomenon of religious ambiguity.

Before proceeding to explore this phenomenon, however, I wish to add a footnote. I said previously that if the Basic Belief Apologetic centers on the existence of a religious belief–generating mechanism, a doubter can say that he or she does not have this mechanism or that it does not work in his or her case; and I suggested that this would involve no violation of doxastic obligations. This can, of course, be contested, and many believers would indeed contest this because they would hold, with Saint Paul and with John Calvin, that everyone is endowed with this belief-forming mechanism and that those who would claim not to have it are deceiving themselves.[38] This claim, however, cannot be supported by the empirical evidence in any straightforward way. It is true that throughout human history it has been rare to find persons or peoples who are devoid of religious beliefs; that we now find widespread unbelief seems the result of the spread of scientific culture and understanding. To show that belief in God is a universal endowment and its apparent absence is the result of its sinful suppression, it is necessary to show both that the welter of polytheistic religious beliefs and practices in the world are in fact perversions of a prior awareness of one God and that the developments that have made so many people disinclined to believe in God today are the result of sin or unwillingness to admit one's faults and not merely the result of a rational inclination to rest content with scientific explanations. Although there are theological reasons to interpret the phenomena in this way, the evidence is clearly not in favor of this interpretation in the majority of cases. Certainly the onus of proof for such an uncharitable and counterintuitive judgment lies squarely with those who make it.

Notes

1. Pascal 1966, 427/194.
2. Ibid., 429/229.
3. Ibid., 427/194.
4. Sextus Empiricus 1933, 25–30.
5. Pascal 1966, 691/432.
6. But see my subsequent discussion on prudential theism.
7. See the Conclusion to Book I of Hume 1978. For comment, see Penelhum 1992b, Chapter 1; and Penelhum 1993.
8. Hume 1978, 416.
9. See, respectively, Pascal 1966, 418/233; Butler 1900, vol. 2; and James 1979.
10. Butler 1900, vol. 2, 149.
11. Penelhum 1985, Chapter 8; and Penelhum 1992a.
12. Butler 1900, vol. 2, 150ff.
13. I differ here from Rescher 1985; and Wernham 1987.
14. Pascal 1966, 419/419.
15. For the first, see Webb 1929, Chapter 5; for the second, see Robinson 1964, 117.
16. Luke 12:16–21.
17. There is a magnificent passage in his meditation on *The Mystery of Christ* that suggests the strongest confidence that the search would be successful. But it would be absurd to think that the argument with the interlocutor in the Wager fragment assumes he is searching in the way spoken of there. Pascal 1966, 314.
18. Article 25. The reference to Paul is to 1 Corinthians 12:23–32.
19. Sermon 15, paragraph 9. See Butler 1900, vol. 1.
20. Penelhum 1964.
21. I explain this concept later.
22. Penelhum 1971a, Chapter 3.
23. Swinburne 1979.
24. Plantinga 1983b.
25. See the Bibliography for full citations.
26. There is some unclarity about the historical figures who are blamed for the demand these apologists reject and about the extension of the term *foundationalist*. Plantinga is inclined to include classical natural theologians such as Aquinas, and even Plato, under the latter label, whereas Wolterstorff emphasizes most especially the influence of Locke.
27. Plantinga 1982, 270.
28. Locke 1959, Book IV, Chapter 19, 13–14.
29. For detailed discussion of the disanalogies between Christian Mystical Practice and Sense Perceptual Doxastic Practice, see Alston 1991, 197–225.

30. Plantinga 1993b, vi.

31. Ibid., 11–17.

32. Reid himself still seemed to think that the rationality of belief in God depended on the success of natural theology; he is criticized for this in Wolterstorff 1983b. See Penelhum 1992c for comment.

33. Alston 1991, 22.

34. For example, Plantinga 1983a, 80. See Alston 1991, 195–197.

35. We might, in comparison, wonder how far the phenomenology of memory requires us to describe it as a flavor of the past appearing to us or how far the distinctive character of the experience of necessity we have when apprehending simple mathematical truths is plausibly rendered in the language of appearing.

36. This statement, I realize, will be contested. I return to it later.

37. Plantinga 1992, 292–293.

38. Paul makes this claim in Romans 1:18–32; Calvin repeats and develops it in Chapters 3–5 of Book I of Calvin 1960. For discussion of Paul's judgments, see Barr 1993, Chapter 3.

CHAPTER SIX

Faith and Ambiguity

We have seen that the decline of the influence of classical foundationalism has enabled defenders of religious faith to argue that it does not need to be supported by independent argument in order to be judged rational. For the mode of acquisition, testing, and sustenance of its core beliefs may well parallel those of many forms of secular commonsense belief that also lack noncircular forms of philosophical justification. This point has been well established by the proponents of the Basic Belief Apologetic. But I have also argued that this apologetic is purely defensive in its force and that it merely shows that the believer may well violate no doxastic obligations. The same could be said of unbelievers. If this statement is accurate, we seem to reach a doxastic stalemate. In the language that John Hick uses, we have to acknowledge the religious ambiguity of the universe.[1] I think the problem that he identifies by this phrase is more complex and wide ranging than he seems to admit, and I try to say why I think so. My comments, however, are confined to aspects of the problem that bear upon the questions to which this book is addressed.

Faith and Naturalism

Hick defines the religious ambiguity of the world by saying it is "capable from our present human vantage point of being thought and experienced in both religious and naturalistic ways."[2] He goes on to say what is surely true: There are those who interpret it in the one way and those who interpret it in the other. Since the widespread naturalism, or religious skepticism, of modern times has developed in societies where the dominant religion has been Christianity, and to a lesser extent Judaism, the form naturalism has taken has been a self-consciously atheistic one. He therefore continues his account of the nature of this ambiguity by contrasting theistic and atheistic worldviews. For the present I follow him in this. What I say here is much the same as what I said on this theme in a book I wrote over twenty years ago.[3] I augment it in the section following.

The believer and the naturalist share a common world, which can be defined adequately for our purposes as a common, scientifically ordered universe that both perceive and interpret in terms of a wide range of shared commonsense doxastic practices of the kind that only an epistemological skeptic is inclined to doubt. They part company, however, at the crucial point where the believer interprets the shared world they inhabit as having a range of significance that the unbeliever does not feel it to have. To the believer it is a world created by God, and guided by him, and in which each of us has a need to restore his or her nature to harmonious relationship with God's purposes for us. To the unbeliever this is an additional interpretation that he or she has no inclination to make. To the believer the unbeliever's doubt represents the subtraction of an all-important dimension of understanding that deprives life of the key to its meaning. Historically speaking, the right language for describing the period of transition to what is now often called the post-Christian era is the language of subtraction; but the language of addition, which makes the believer's stance a minority complication, is probably a statistically more accurate way of speaking about the cultural situation in which we find ourselves now at the end of this transition. The transition is commonly described as a process of secularization. To express the matter neutrally: The believer and the unbeliever share a common world, but to the believer the world is what it seems to the unbeliever to be but is more besides. The believer's additions seem gratuitous to the unbeliever (hence the easy appeal of the evidentialist thesis that there really ought to be independent evidence of what the believer adds); the unbeliever's world, though shared by the believer in an obvious way in daily affairs, seems nevertheless to the believer to be an empty, anxiety-ridden, and even absurd world. The unbeliever, in a disagreement that we have encountered before, concedes the reality of many of the evils that the believer sees, including many in our own natures, but does not concede the reality of those that are supposed to follow from alienation from God.[4]

The world's evils are worse to the believer than to the unbeliever; for every agreed fault in the world or in ourselves is also an offense against God, and every fault in ourselves is due to our unwillingness to submit to his will. This greater pessimism about our unregenerate condition is matched, however, by a far greater optimism about the possibilities of a future restored by a reconciliation with God. To the unbeliever the believer's pessimism is pathological, and the believer's optimism is utopian; and he judges each to be a major psychological hindrance to the serious secular business of seeing to it that the evils it is in our power to ameliorate are dealt with.

These two worldviews can, and do, coexist in a shared world. Even though it seems to matter infinitely who is right, and even though one's stance on this question can affect almost every detail of life, it does not seem that either can convict the other of failing to meet doxastic obligations. The success of the Basic Belief Apologetic serves, in my view, to accentuate this ambiguity, not reduce it. For it shows that the believer cannot be convicted of irrationality for not providing the sort of evidence that would convince the unbeliever to believe. Of course, the believer will see his or her own doxastic inclinations as due to divine grace. But this view does nothing to show that the unbeliever, who lacks this inclination, is irrational to be without it or irrational in judging the believer to be following a doxastic mechanism that aims at comfort rather than truth.

To show that this stalemate is a real one, let us consider two related moves that parallel the evidentialist challenge from the believer's side. The believer may feel that unbelievers are refusing to see the deeper significance of their shared world and that greater openness to the insights of the faith would change this. Unbelievers should permit their latent theistic belief–generating mechanism to function. Those who try to activate it are, of course, the preachers; and unbelievers should give them a hearing. But why should unbelievers allow themselves to be preached at? For preachers are people who put others under the sort of emotional stress that undermines

their judgment and plays on their fears. On matters of great importance one should withhold decision until one is calm, properly fed
and rested, and able to assess matters detachedly. To decide whether
this is a good reason for staying away from preachers is to decide
what is or is not the right frame of mind in which to meet reality,
and this is not a decision that is neutral between these two worldviews. The demand for religious openness looks like a mere theistic
counterpart to the evidentialist demand for proofs.

A related and more promising theistic response is to be found in
the claim that we find in Saint Paul and in John Calvin: that all human beings are in fact endowed with an awareness of God and that
if they deny his reality, they are in fact denying something that they
already know.[5] Unbelief, on this view, is self-deception. If this claim
is true, then no one is without the faith-generating doxastic mechanism, and the unbeliever merely suppresses it through sin—that is,
through reluctance to concede obligations to God and a wish to go
on living as though he is not there.

It must be said, first, that the evidence is, on the surface, against
any such claim since if we look around us in the post-Christian age,
there are many who claim to have no inclination to believe at all.
Some even wish they had, or say so. If the claim is true, then they
are guilty, through sin, of suppressing the inclination they claim not
to have. The claim would not be shown to be true merely by the
fact, if it were one, that those who claimed to be without this doxastic inclination had anxieties and moral problems of which faith
would be a cure since that could be the case if the doxastic inclination they seem to lack would merely serve comfort rather than
truth. Of course, the sickness and spiritual alienation of the modern
world are commonly blamed on its godlessness, and this may be the
main reason for them. But this, too, can be argued by the unbeliever
to show at most that faith would help cure us, not that its core beliefs are true.

In addition, the actual anthropological evidence seems to indicate that, although belief in what Hume called "invisible, intelligent
power" is enormously widespread, it has most commonly taken an-
imistic and polytheistic forms, and monotheistic beliefs seem to
have developed from these.[6] If they are still judged to be corrupt or
primitive versions of a universal human belief in God, this judgment can only be the result of reading latter-day monotheism into
them. I incline, therefore, to say that the Pauline-Calvinian thesis of

a universal human doxastic inclination toward belief in God, which is corrupted through sin, is empirically false. But even if the evidence that seems to count against it can be explained in ways that are consistent with it, I judge that the Paul-Calvin thesis gets its plausibility from within the scheme of faith and is not independent of it.

If this account of the stalemate between faith and naturalism is thus far correct, then we have to recognize that there seem to be no common standards of rationality that either side violates in its opposition to the other. It is true that each side has difficulties to contend with that the other side does not. In Plantinga's language, each has to contend with potential defeaters. The believing side has to contend with more of these because its worldview is more complex: It is only the believer who has to face the problem of evil, for example, since the evils the unbeliever also admits to exist are not evils that the unbeliever sees as existing in a world governed by divine goodness. But the unbeliever has potential defeaters, too. Most noticeably, there is the problem of accounting for those special religious phenomena on which Alston's apologetic centers, and of which the naturalistic accounts do seem to be strained and implausible. Of course, each side has to say something to explain the sheer fact of doxastic difference; each has to explain why rational beings exist on the other side. But the resources for this endeavor are, in each case, plentiful enough: The believer can be accused of pathological guilt, fear of the unknown, and an unrealistic optimism about our capacity for moral change; and the unbeliever can be accused of buying explanatory economy at the price of superficiality and of displaying an unwillingness to admit the depth of our moral needs. Such explanations gain their plausibility only within the worldviews they are used to support. This does not mean that they are all false, but it does mean that each has its parallel on the other side.

To live in a religiously ambiguous world is to live, then, in a world where a theistic worldview and an atheistic worldview are both rational. It is important to notice here that if one of the traditional forms of natural theology were successful, we would *not* live in an ambiguous world. For an ambiguous world is one that it is rational to interpret in both ways. But if God's being, goodness, and providential care could be proved to be realities, then this would mean that for those who were aware of the relevant arguments, atheism would not be a rational option. Religious ambiguity is not a matter merely of the existence of both theists and atheists; it is a matter of its being rational to be both, and in a world where it was proved that God exists, those who knew this had been done would not be rational to be atheists. The same would be true in reverse if it had been proved that God does not exist; in such a world theism would not be a rational option for someone who knew this had been proved. But in the absence of such disambiguation, we seem to have to accept that we live in a world that can be interpreted in both these incompatible ways by rational beings, in which their disagreement is itself subsumable under each of the two worldviews, and in which the transition from one view to the other involves what Kierkegaard calls a leap, and Hick describes as an apperceptive shift, that can be explained in the language of each position but has weight only within the scheme that the convert enters, not the one he or she has left.

The Faiths and Their Competitors

This understanding of the world's ambiguity now seems to me far too restricted and parochial. It is a monocultural account that ignores, in the first place, the major diversities among the religions of the world. It assumes that the world's ambiguity is between a Christian, or perhaps a Jewish, interpretation of it and a naturalistic one. The thinkers of the Enlightenment, whichever side they were on, did indeed make this assumption. William Paley, for example, in his *Evidences of Christianity*, begins with the following statement:

> I deem it unnecessary to prove that mankind stood in need of a revelation, because I have met with no serious person who thinks that, even under the Christian revelation, we have too much light, or any degree of assurance which is superfluous. I desire moreover, that in judging of Christianity, it may be remembered, that the question lies between this religion and none: for if the Christian religion be not credible, no one, with whom we have to do, will support the pretensions of any other.[7]

Fortunately or not we now "have to do" with a wider circle than Paley thought he had to consider, and such comments as his would today be judged unrealistic, if not outrageous. For growth in communication and an enormous increase in scholarly understanding have combined to produce a cultural situation in which religious traditions that seemed remote or exotic in Paley's day are now open and live options to many who would indeed have been confronted in the past with a choice between Christianity and some kind of naturalism. For some in Europe or North America transplanted offshoots of Hindu or Buddhist traditions represent genuine choices in a world where the Christian faith seems unbelievable and a naturalist worldview impossibly bleak or superficial. An understanding of the world's ambiguity therefore has to allow for the fact that there are other religious traditions that compete for the adherence of the rational being with the forms of faith we have been examining hitherto.

Those who study the major religious traditions of the world (the ones that John Hick, following Jaspers, refers to as the postaxial religions[8]) are often struck by both their similarities (which Hick emphasizes) and their deep differences. Their similarities, which enable us to see them as species of a genus, can be spelled out in a very broad way that I think is adequate for our present argument. Each is soteriological; that is to say, each offers us a way of salvation or liberation from a predicament that it diagnoses and that, for reasons it will have ready to describe, we are unwilling to recognize. The predicament is said, in each case, to arise because our mode of life at the level of common sense and common aspiration is alienated from a deeper, or transcendent, reality with which we prefer not to relate. The three great Western faiths identify this reality with a personal God, and the predicament of our situation is judged by them to be the result of disobedience to his will and rejection of his love.

The various forms of the two great Eastern traditions of Hinduism and Buddhism, while containing many elements that resemble the piety and worship of the Western faiths, do not judge the human predicament or its causes in the same way. Buddhism is overtly atheistic, and at least some of the dominant strands in Hinduism maintain that the ultimate spiritual reality of the cosmos is not personal, though it may have personal manifestations. The core diagnosis of human ills in these traditions is that they are due to ignorance concerning our individual relationship to the cosmos; this ignorance invests our own selfhood with a reality and a separateness that are manufactured and illusory. The sufferings that result from unsatisfied human craving are consequences of ascribing separate reality and importance to this self, from which it may take a pilgrimage of many lives to be liberated. Each of us has begun this present life with a karmic legacy of previous choices that determines how far from this ultimate liberation we find ourselves.

Since the diagnosis of the human predicament is different, the prescriptions offered for its cure differ also. Since the Western faiths see salvation as a divine gift that follows on moral transformation, their prescriptions, though not all identical, have a common core: an acceptance of the need for individual repentance and request for divine mercy and a trust in the promises God has made to those who submit and try to do his will. To the Jew and the Muslim, this submission entails a joyous, not a reluctant, adoption of a way of life that to outsiders seems filled with irksome restrictions but that to the faithful contains paths toward being accounted righteous in the sight of God. To the Christian this way of life entails a recognition that each person needs the particular saving grace and intervention of Christ to atone for the chronic shortcomings of his or her attempts to do what God wishes. The essence of each tradition, therefore, is faith in the proclamations that the believer considers God has made to those who turn from a self-centered life to a life centered on the will of God.

But when the ills of human life are seen as consequences of ignorance or misperception, then the cure for this cannot consist solely in reformation of conduct or a cleansing from guilt, though these will certainly have their place as part of the path toward liberation and as consequences of its attainment. Moral reformation is seen in the last resort as subordinate to the cure for ignorance, namely, enlightenment. This fundamental divergence among the world's religious traditions entails a different picture of the saved or liberated personality: the personality that has been through the fires of religious change and can be viewed as a light and example to others. In the Western faiths this person is the righteous or saintly personality, the one who is morally oriented toward union with God. In the great Eastern traditions the liberated person is the guru, arhat, or enlightened one who has achieved severance from the illusory satisfactions and pains of desire and self-indulgence and has come to realize (in both senses) his or her ultimate identity with the way things are.

A consequence of the divergence in diagnosis and prescription is a divergence in religious phenomenology. The experiences of the key formative figures of the Western tradition are of the holiness and righteousness of God or of his love. They are experiences that do not lessen the creature's sense of dependence and relative insignificance over against the God who calls or judges or forgives. The key experiences of the Eastern religions are of emptying individual separateness; they are experiences of what Alston calls absolute immediacy. Insofar as moral change is enjoined on the convert, it is enjoined as a path (albeit a path that may last through many lives) that will issue in such experience, not as an end in itself. This phenomenological divergence has led Ninian Smart, for example, to distinguish sharply between the numinous and the mystical strands in religion.

The varying usages of the word *mystical* is a source of much scholarly argument. There are those, following W. T. Stace, who think that all mystical experience has to be assessed and classified against a paradigm of absolute immediacy, so that any experience in which the subject does not feel absorbed into the cosmic reality in which he or she is participating is only an imperfect approximation of the mystical. This makes the experiences of the large numbers of theistic mystics in the West only imperfectly mystical ones, a judgment that is hotly contested by Zaehner and most recently by Michael Stoeber. If Stace is right, Alston is misusing the term *mystical* to describe the supposed encounters with God that many Christians claim, regardless of whether they would classify themselves as mystics.[9] (It is not trivial to note that the mystics of the Jewish, Christian, and Islamic faiths, though often revered, are not central to those faiths and their development in the way in which figures such as Gautama or Sankara are central to the development of the Eastern traditions. Western mystics have sometimes been objects of suspicion also; Protestant Christianity has been far less receptive to the mystic life than the Catholic tradition, for example.)

But this debate, though important, need not detain us here. It is enough to note that there are some dominant forms of Eastern religious life and practice that center upon the search for a form of religious experience that does not lend itself to interpretations that are consistent with the teachings of the Western faiths or offer a cure for the same core defect in human personality. Such experience is also believed to transcend doctrinal statement and therefore to transcend any state in which belief is at the core, even though it seems incoherent to suggest that one can consciously enter on a path that is directed toward such experience without being prompted to do so by initial beliefs about the release to which this path will lead.

To enter on one of these forms of life and practice, then, is to begin with at least a provisional or inherited acceptance of a scheme of understanding of human nature and its needs and to follow a path that deepens and reinforces that understanding and controls opinion and choice in the interest of seeking liberation from the ills it identifies. In doing all this, the adherent of one of these traditions seems clearly to be following a set of doxastic practices that are as clearly rational, and as free from failures of doxastic obligation, as the path of the Jew, Christian, or Muslim.

Each of these various religious traditions can, and does, make judgments about the paths advocated by the others; and each can, and does, make judgments about the secular world and those who choose to live wholly within its spiritual confines. Hick is, however, correct to stress that the detailed confrontation that Western history has engendered between Christianity and Judaism, on the one hand, and atheistic naturalism, on the other, has yet to develop in as extensive and detailed a form between each of these traditions and a correspondingly desupernaturalized worldview in the East.

This brief and schematic glance at the nature of some of the major religious alternatives to the Western faiths shows us that the religious ambiguity of the world is a far more complex matter than if we concentrate solely upon the confrontation between any one of the Western faiths and the secular naturalism with which it coexists. We live in a world that is characterized by *multiple* religious ambiguity. In that world each religion is inclined to judge the others as being approximations to itself or as manifesting some or all of the spiritual weaknesses that it diagnoses in the human condition. The Buddhist may see the advaitist Hindu as failing to transcend selfhood but reinflating it by interpeting mystic union as an identification of the atman (or inner self) with Brahman; the advaitist may see the theistic faiths as failing to see devotion to a deity as merely a partial step toward self-transcendence; the Christian may judge the Mahayana Buddhist's concept of the bodhisattva, who remains on this side of final enlightenment through compassion, as nothing better than a confused acknowledgment of the need for Christ. Judgments of this sort, even when accompanied (as they often, notoriously, are not) by charity and imagination, seem patronizing and uncomprehending to those who are their targets, but good reasons can be given for them within the traditions that prompt them.

Some traditions are more easygoing about their competitors than others are. The Hindu is apt to baffle others by accepting Christ, Moses, and other spiritual figures of the West as manifestations of the same, ultimately impersonal, cosmic power, whereas the Christian usually makes exclusive claims about the nature of the work of Christ that repudiates such an acceptance as a mere refusal to face our need for what he has done. The important point for our present purpose is that such mutual judgments are expressions of principles that are themselves internal to the system from within which they are made. And each will see the doxastic mechanisms of the others as aimed at something less than the combination of truth and liberation/salvation that its own is aimed at and as deriving from a failure to confront the real source of ill of which its own system informs us.

This ambiguity has always existed, if it exists now. But in past eras, when interaction and mutual knowledge were so much harder to attain, the sort of partisan judgment passed by William Paley was excusable, and the ambiguity could pass unnoticed. The world can be ambiguous, and in the past was ambiguous, without uninformed persons knowing this. And the fact that very many people in the world are firmly of the view that a particular Christian, Jewish, Islamic, or Buddhist (or naturalistic) interpretation of it is true, and can see no merit in the competition, does not show that it is not ambiguous now; it shows only that they do not see that it is.

So the ambiguity that pervades the relationship between the faiths and their naturalistic competition also pervades the relationship among the major religious traditions of the world. And it is an ambiguity that, though it does not take away from the doxastic propriety of each believer and indeed is a result of it, nevertheless seems to present us with a reason for anxiety about whether any believer has warrant for his or her commitment. One is reminded here of the Tenth Mode of classical Skepticism, "the one depending on lifestyles and customs and laws and belief in myth and dogmatic suppositions," which led the Skeptic to suspend judgment about our capacity to arrive at truth in such matters.[10] Although we have seen many reasons for not supposing that such suspension is possible, or that it is a rational response to the anxiety that the variety of religious opinion may cause, the anxiety itself is at least an intelligible result of recognizing the reasons so many believers have for believing the incompatible things they do.

Let us call this dimension of the ambiguity of the world its interreligious ambiguity. To describe it in this language is to pinpoint the epistemological difficulties that attend a recognition of what scholars of religion refer to as religious pluralism. These are difficulties that beset any argument, such as the Basic Belief Apologetic, that centers on the epistemic propriety of the belief-forming mechanisms of one religious tradition. What it tells us about the tradition of those who use it can be said about other traditions. This is a problem in which Christian apologists continue to show very little sustained interest, being more exclusively concerned to fend off the challenges of secular naturalism. There have been exceptions to this, however, and I wish to comment on them briefly.

The most widely discussed work in this field is that of John Hick, whose distinguished career has been notable for his sustained insistence on the religious and philosophical importance of exploring the implications of the increased understanding now available about the major religious traditions of humanity. His own explorations of them have reached their most sustained and elegant expression in *An Interpretation of Religion.*[11] I cannot begin to attempt a response to this work here but merely try to show how it offers us one possible way of dealing with the challenge presented to the rational inquirer by the world's bewildering religious variety.

Hick makes no attempt to downplay the deep doctrinal differences among the great postaxial religions. They differ over such apparent fundamentals as the nature of human alienation and the nature of the ultimate reality to which human beings normally fail to relate. The alienation is said by some to be due to sin, by others to be due to ignorance; the ultimate cosmic reality is said by some to be a transcendent personal God and by others to be an immanent impersonal spiritual power. Even though they all offer salvation or liberation, to some this is the final fulfillment of the deepest aspirations of the individual soul, and to others it entails the cessation of individuality. But in spite of these deep differences, Hick declines to take refuge in nonrealist theories that seek some ultimate concord by passing over the claims that believers make about the cosmos we inhabit. He offers instead a different interpretation of religion: "Having, then, rejected . . . the skeptical view that religious experience is *in toto* delusory, and the dogmatic view that it is all delusory except that of one's own tradition, I propose to explore the third possibility that the great post-axial faiths constitute different ways of experiencing, conceiving and living in relation to an ultimate divine Reality which transcends all our varied versions of it."[12] He offers us a theory, Kantian in character, in which he distinguishes between the Real as it is in itself and the real as it appears to, or is experienced by, human beings. The great religions are culturally determined modes of experiencing a Real that appears to all but is experienced by each in a culturally relative manner that generates mutually incompatible doctrinal understandings.

The major benefit of such an interpretation is that it enables us, if we follow it, to ascribe a veridical character to traditions other than our own without supposing that the traditions themselves are all saying and demanding the same things or interpreting the Real in ways that are not really different. The ultimate answer to anyone who asks, within one such tradition, why he or she should think any other tradition could be veridical is that the denial of this cannot survive open encounter with the highest manifestations of the spirituality of those other traditions.

The limitations of the present work do not permit me to delve into the implications, or the difficulties, of this interpretation, which are only beginning to be explored. I can offer only a few remarks on the way it impinges on my own present argument about faith and ambiguity. I have suggested that understanding the world's ambiguity in terms of a stark contrast between faith and naturalism ignores the additional dimension of religious ambiguity. If Hick's interpretation is fundamentally correct, then we can say that religious ambiguity, though certainly a feature of human experience (and indeed one that he emphasizes), is more superficial than the ambiguity between the great religions and secular naturalism. For secular naturalism denies something that in their different ways all the great religions, on this interpretation of them, affirm: There is a transcendent reality that manifests itself to us in religious experience and that, in manifesting itself to us there, offers us salvation or liberation from the dissatisfactions and anxieties of self-centered living. For all the deep differences of teaching, all the great religions offer us the chance of reorientation of personality, escape from anxiety, and a vision of human possibilities that transcends the limits of the person's present life. It is only naturalism that confines us to that present life, that denies these wider possibilities, and that thinks the very concept of personal salvation is merely utopian.

I think the appeal of an interpretation like Hick's is considerable since it at least offers a potential line of apologetic for the defender of one of the Western faiths who is concerned by the implications of the spiritual authenticity of other traditions, and it provides in advance an apologetic option that might well help arm the apologist of another tradition that has not yet confronted naturalistic challenges. But I have two difficulties. The first, to which I return later, is that this way of dealing with religious ambiguity oversimplifies the complexities of present-day naturalistic thought, which is no more monolithic in its spiritual implications than religious thought is. The second is that an interpretation like Hick's, which assumes that actual religious life will always continue to be marked by the same divisions that we find in it now, or at least by some of them, and is not offered as a base for some amorphous world religion, is bound to have the effect of diluting the commitment adherents who accept it have to their own faith. If I come to think that the tradition I adhere to has rational grounds, but that it is paralleled in this respect by other traditions that can account for it in their own terms as it can account for them, this second-order realization can hardly fail to affect the degree and manner of my participation. Indeed, to some extent this realization is intended to reduce the need to proselytize among other postaxial traditions and to explain the relative lack of success of missionary attempts to do so. But the sorts of reasons that can lead to this consequence are also the sorts of reasons that cannot fail to suggest that *my own* faith commitment may have no more ultimate validity than its competitors suggest it has.

The impact of second-order theories on first-order commitments is an intriguing and complex topic. Some think, for example, that the emotive theory of ethics, if accepted, would undermine the moral commitments it seeks to analyze, although whether this is so is hard to determine. Some second-order theories, such as those of Freudian psychotherapy, are indeed intended to weaken the hold of the practices they analyze. I admit to being very uncertain how far a theory like that of John Hick can leave the actual practice of religious faith as it is or whether it is bound to introduce a degree of inner reservation into the religious life that must weaken it. There are those who would think that this sort of weakening would be religiously beneficial, but I confess to being unclear here also.

Hick's "field theory" of religion responds to religious ambiguity by suggesting that the variations, and incompatibilities, in belief among the main religions of the world are differing responses to one and the same ultimate transcendent reality. A somewhat similar stance is adopted by Wilfred Cantwell Smith in two important works, *Faith and Belief,* and *Belief and History.*[13] The implications of Smith's thesis for the problem that presently confronts us are radical ones. He seeks to demolish the contemporary assumption that faith is belief-plus. He maintains that faith is found in all the major religious traditions and is a common feature of those human beings who belong to them. It is a positive response to transcendent reality and a willingness to devote one's life to serving it; it is not what belief is, namely (on Smith's view), the adoption of one of a competing sea of opinions on this or that doctrinal matter. Faith is a worldwide constant and involves the reorientation of the whole personality, whereas belief can be warm or tepid, firm or tentative, and manifestly variable from culture to culture.

The obsession with belief in present-day discussions of religion (of which this book is no doubt one example) is, in addition, the result of an evolution in the idea of belief itself. With unmatched learning and ingenuity, Smith shows how the use of the word *believe* and its cognates has moved from earlier uses in which they expressed devotion or commitment toward their present-day function of expressing the adoption of doctrine or opinion. "I believe . . . " did not originally mean "I am of the opinion that . . . " but "I hold dear . . . " or "I pledge myself to . . . " The word's original religious function (as in the language of the Christian creeds) was to express *faith,* that is, a wholehearted reorientation toward a transcendent reality whose being is presupposed and not stated. Whereas the object of belief in the modern sense is propositions, the object of belief in the term's original sense is the liberating reality to which believers dedicate themselves.[14] It is this, and not opinion, that is faith, and it is "an essential human quality, a normal if priceless component of what it means to be a human person."[15] Faced with the obvious diversity of worldviews among the religious traditions of the world, it is a "monumental error" to seek "similarity of belief—or as much of it as can be salvaged or contrived—rather than similarity of faith."[16]

I do not attempt here to offer a view on how far Smith's position is the same as John Hick's, although the similarity of motive is clear in one central respect: Each seeks to emphasize the deep unity of the religious life while recognizing the immense variety of cosmic understandings to be found within it. I instead make one or two comments on what I think is the bearing of his views on the arguments I have presented here. The first and most obvious point to note is that Smith is clearly in that tradition of Christian scholarship that deplores the emphasis of Christian thought on doctrinal orthodoxy at the expense of other dimensions of faith. If what is central to Christian faith is the espousal of the right doctrines, then the path is paved to the excesses of inquisitorial heresy-hunting and to the outright rejection of the spiritual riches of the other religious traditions with which Christianity shares the planet and to which it has responded so often with ignorant hostility.

This defect is not always attributed to the influence of modern secularism, however, although this is the source that Smith blames. For example, Edwin Hatch blames this chronic feature of Christian thought on the influence of Greek philosophical schools on the development of the early Christian church. He deplores this influence in the following terms:

> There is no more reason to suppose that God has revealed metaphysics than that He has revealed chemistry. The Christian revelation is, at least primarily, a setting forth of certain facts. It does not in itself afford a guarantee of the certainty of the speculations which are built upon those facts. All such speculations are *dogmas* in the original sense of the word. They are simply personal convictions. . . . The belief that metaphysical theology is more than this, is the chief bequest of Greece to religious thought, and it has been a *damnosa hereditas*. It has given to later Christianity that part of it which is doomed to perish, and which yet, while it lives, holds the key of the prison-house of many souls.[17]

Hatch wrote these words in 1888, at a time when many Christians saw doctrinal concerns as far too dominant in relation to the ethical dynamic of their faith. But their judgment coincides with a recognition that Christianity has always emphasized the acceptance of its core truths more crucially than Judaism and Islam, in which faith is expressed far more in what is called orthopraxy rather than orthodoxy: the doing of what God demands rather than the acknowledgment of what God says. What Hatch and Smith share, very obviously, is an intense conviction that faith is more than mere acknowledgment.

But however far we agree to this, we have also to recognize that the reality to which adherents of all religious traditions respond is apprehended in ways that are inevitably propositional to some important degree. Hatch recognizes this in calling them "facts," and Smith also concedes this in speaking of them as presupposed in faith. Here we confront a fact that has been acknowledged throughout the history of modern philosophy: We all presuppose many things that philosophers articulate for us and that skeptics have questioned. It will indeed be odd for us to include them in our list of *opinions*, but philosophers have commonly included them in their lists of our beliefs. When philosophers like myself speak of the beliefs that are at the core of faith, they include not only the stated doctrines that are pronounced in the recitation of the creed, or the interpretations of these developed by theologians, but also the presuppositions about the cosmos to which those doctrines and interpretations are responses. For example, when Plantinga refers to the experiences and intimations that give the grounds for the basic beliefs of Christians, he points out that they are experiences of God's anger or forgiveness and that the *existence* of God is more properly thought of as inferrable from the beliefs about God's anger or forgiveness than as a distinct basic belief in its own right.[18] But it would be quixotic to deduce from this that Christians do not believe that God exists.

There is a terminological issue here, though not a trivial one. It is true that when we ask some eminent personage what his or her beliefs are, we are likely to be asking about that person's convictions on important moral or social questions; it would be odd for that person to start responding by listing all, or even any, of the truisms that G. E. Moore insists he knows in the *Defence of Common Sense*, such as "The earth has existed for many years past."[19] However, it would not be at all odd for that person to say nowadays, "I believe there is a God," because many do not believe this. Thus far Smith is right: We tend in present-day parlance to use the word *belief* to refer to the acceptance of propositions on matters of importance that divide us, not to refer to matters on which we all take the same facts for granted. But once we concede (and how can we not?) that the adherents of the great religions of the world take different things for granted, and that these things are not taken for granted by adherents of other traditions or by the nonreligious, the standard philosophical extension of the word *belief* to include these presuppositions seems the only viable procedure.

I have assumed this in speaking of these presuppositions as forming the doxastic core of faith. And there is such a doxastic core for every faith: It is that apprehension of the world that must be present for the response of the faith to be formulated and entered into by the believer. It is true that Christianity, more than other faiths, has emphasized that that response includes the acceptance of certain understandings of what ails us, what will cure us, what our destiny is, and who Jesus is. This emphasis contrasts (self-consciously) with the emphasis on detailed practice characteristic of the two great law-centered faiths: Judaism and Islam. But this does not show that they are innocent of beliefs, for their practical demands indeed presuppose such beliefs. The matter has been confused by the fact that this difference has so often been put by saying that Christianity emphasizes faith rather than works. But this is, at worst, a misleading way of stating that the relative importance of the distinguishable elements in faith that we discussed in Chapter 4 differs from one faith to another and does not show that one has a doxastic core when the others do not or that none has.

There is another nontrivial question about nomenclature that Smith's study raises for us. In analyzing the philosophical problems generated by religious faith, I have consciously emphasized the theistic religious traditions and have put to one side the question of how far it is proper to use the same language to describe the religious traditions that are not (or are not ultimately) theistic. These traditions also represent responses to a presupposed understanding of reality, present us with a diagnosis of the human condition that needs to be accepted for the response to be made, and offer their adherents release from the shackles that the diagnosis is thought to reveal. They have a doxastic core, a life path in response to our perceived predicament, and a soteriological hope. Are they, therefore, *faiths?*

There is no doubt that on Smith's view they are since faith is the human response that is common to all the traditions. It is interesting to note that he chooses to make his case by starting with the most obvious apparent counterinstance, namely, Buddhism, which is overtly atheistic. Noting that some Western interpreters have found the concept of Nirvana analogous to that of God, he suggests that a better analogy with the object of the theist's faith is to be found in the concept of the Dharma, the saving way of life that leads to Nirvana. It is "the one eternal principle in a universe otherwise chaotic."[20] What constitutes the faith of the Buddha's followers is the choice to follow Dharma (which he did not invent but discovered) in assurance that it will ultimately lead to release. This view makes faith essentially a reorientation of life toward liberation believed to have a transcendent source, though not necessarily a personal one. All the great religions of the world qualify for the title of faiths thus interpreted—provided, at least, that the transcendent source can be found within as well as beyond the consciousness of the seeker. The affective component is some form of driving confidence that liberation will indeed be the outcome.

It is only possible on such a matter to give reasons for a preference, not to prove the incorrectness of a different one. If faith is understood this broadly, then the analysis of it that I have offered is clearly unduly narrow. I have taken faith to be a response to supposed revelation and the affective and conative components in it to be found in the trust in the being believed to have given the revelation. The expectation of salvation is the source of the serenity characteristic of lived faith so understood. But on this view of faith, even works-centered faith, the salvation is given rather than achieved. It may be felt within, but it is bestowed from without. In this I have followed Kierkegaard in drawing a contrast between responding to God in faith and learning from the secular teacher, of whom the paradigm is Socrates.

Socrates draws the student to discover truth within. It is there already, waiting to be uncovered beneath the dross and lumber of confusion and egocentricity. The student does not merely have to submit and say yes; the student has to uncover it by whatever grinding work and self-analysis are necessary. The way of the enlightenment religions is long and hard, however sudden the end may be; and the end is already within, waiting to be found there. The enlightenment religions are far more like the Western secular philosophy that was fathered by Socrates than they are like the three great Semitic faiths; and the chronic tensions between the demands of philosophy and those of faith are not as characteristic of their histories. Although I do not draw many of the conclusions from Kierkegaard's contrast that he draws, the contrast itself seems

to be profoundly correct and to be an overriding reason to refrain
from calling "faiths" those religious traditions that seek enlightenment through the inner realization of one's true self. So when
Socrates tells us that no harm can come to the good man (the one,
that is, who cares for the well-being of his own soul above all), this
is not an expression of faith but of a confidence born of a supposed
self-knowledge. The enlightenment of the Eastern sage and the
arhat is like this.

Religion and Naturalism

I have argued so far that the epistemological stalemate between each
of the theistic faiths and naturalism does not exhaust the ambiguity
of the world and that this also is a function of the religious pluralism that is such a well-recognized fact of our cultural life. Each of
the major religious traditions seems prima facie to represent a rational option that violates no doxastic duties and can justify itself in
relation to each of the others, which it can subsume under its own
canons of criticism. Each can challenge, and can be challenged by,
secular naturalism.

But this analysis still does not tell us the whole story. For we
must not ignore the variety of naturalistic understandings of our
world or the ways in which this variety complicates our epistemological map. We can notice, first, that there are naturalisms with
a soteriological cast that parallels that of the major religions. Although these naturalisms reject the transcendent dimension, inner
or outer, that is the source of the demand and the liberation offered
by the great religions, they still claim to have a form of diagnosis of
the human condition and a path to freedom from the ills they discern within it. The most obvious examples of soteriological naturalism in our era are Marxism and Freudianism. Each has a diagnosis
that common sense is reluctant to accept and is inclined to ridicule:
that we are alienated from our true selves through servitude to a
distorted and destructive relationship to the means of production;
that we are hindered by anxiety-driven compulsions that mask sup-
pressed forms of displacement of instinctual energies. Each offers a
demanding but liberating path toward freedom from the burdens
that we labor under and that we are reluctant to admit we carry, a
path that releases its adherents' spiritual energies in ways that help
them deal with their real problems and shed self-imposed ones. It

seems likely that Freudianism and Marxism will shortly be joined by some form of biologically based "Green" ideology that will point us toward fulfillment through acceptance of our affinity with the other species of the planet and a recognition of the genetically programmed character of our natures as sociobiological thought reveals this to us.

So naturalism can and does take on a saving form and offers personal transformation and apperceptive shift just as religion can. Some would say that naturalisms that make claims like this are, for this reason, to be classed as religions.[21] Even though this claim can suggest fruitful ways of understanding the movements thus described, there seems no reason to broaden the notion of a religion to include them. They can, of course, offer their own subsumptions of the aspirations and experiences of the religious life: that religion is the opiate of the masses, that faith is displaced and unacknowledged Oedipal conflict, that religion is a form of speciesism, and so forth. In their turn they can be seen as corrupted or emasculated versions of the quest for restoration of the right relationship to God.

Naturalism may not take a soteriological form, of course, and often does not. Even in systematic theoretical versions, such as classical atomism and its long series of materialist successors, naturalism may merely teach us that the claims of religion are dispensable additional sources of anxiety and fear and that the steady march of science will continue to eliminate the dark corners of ignorance that cause people to resort to religious explanations of what they do not yet understand.[22] And there are naturalists who are reticent about all forms of metaphysics and seek to help us deal with the anxieties of human life by freeing us from the very search for meaning and in-depth understanding that the religions, and the soteriological naturalisms, tell us will cure those anxieties. The best examples of this form of therapeutic naturalism are classical Skepticism and its modern counterparts in Montaigne and, above all, Hume.[23] They teach us to accept our limitations and not torture ourselves by exaggerating them and then adopting heroic measures to overcome them.

My purpose in retailing all these variations is to urge that we do not merely live in a world that exhibits a theist-atheist ambiguity, or one that exhibits religious ambiguity, but one that exhibits multiple religious and ideological ambiguity. The situation that the Basic

Belief Apologetic has taught us to recognize is one in which it is possible to hold and sustain belief in God without having external proofs and justifications and without violating doxastic duties. But this situation is one in which atheists also look to be free of that fault, as we have seen. And it is one in which the adherents of a great many religions, and those of a great many nonreligious systems of thought, are free of that fault too. Believers are too apt to see nothing but nihilism, spiritual drift, and heedlessness around them, but the same rationality that they rightly claim for themselves is all around them as well.

Ambiguity in a Pluralistic Culture

The fact that the adherents of traditions other than one's own may also be rational beings with clear doxastic consciences often needs to be learned. One of the less-heralded benefits of the study of philosophy is the ability it gives those with a modicum of imagination to understand the reasons that can be offered within alien systems of thought for opinions and interpretations that may seem outlandish from a distance but do indeed have their rationale. Most philosophy students encounter opinions like this as they read the classics of their subject, and the ability to understand how such views can arise for reasonable persons is one of philosophy's great legacies for those who are taught it well. The same is true for the comparative study of religion. Its students come not only to learn what interpretations of human life and society are embodied in traditions they do not themselves belong to, but also to acquire an understanding of the reasons that can be given for these interpretations from within those traditions. In most North American universities students are quite likely to have adherents of those traditions in the same classroom and to come to recognize that their own hitherto-unexamined beliefs can be understood in parallel ways.

The value of philosophy and the comparative study of religions to each other cannot be exaggerated. But the essential moral for our purposes is that the enlargement of the imagination that both disciplines can provide enables those of us who live in a culturally pluralistic society to transcend the stance of mere tolerance for the weird private worldviews of our fellows and to understand how and why the world seems to them the sort of place they judge it to be. This involves not merely conceding that one's competitors are rational but also being able in the imagination to participate in their thought processes. It is a teacher's pedagogical duty to encourage the development of this capacity and to attempt to encourage it without nurturing the soft relativism that sometimes accompanies it among the intellectually unwary.

This capacity to participate in thought in the worldviews of others, religious or not, and the correlative capacity to see one's own predispositions in the light of those other views turn the multiple ambiguity of the world into a felt reality for those who acquire them. Our culture prides itself on its ability to nurture them. But they come at the price of self-doubt. For is not the ambiguity of the world itself a reason for hesitation about the truth of each of the views that combine to compose it?

Philosophy and Disambiguation

If the world is ambiguous in this way, how ought we to respond to this fact? I begin with two possible responses that should be dismissed.

1. The first, which we have already touched upon in another connection, is the claim, made most commonly from within a faith, that since the great faiths demand acknowledgment of faults and a willingness to seek personal transformation, hesitation in the face of the faith's claims is due to an unwillingness to make this acknowledgment and follow through on the need for change. In the epistemological language we have used hitherto, what seems to be honest bewilderment in the face of a number of plausible options is in fact a disguised refusal to bestir oneself spiritually.

Although there is no need to deny, and indeed every reason to assert, that the hesitations of many individuals may be due to bad faith of this sort, and although the pervasiveness of self-deception is widely recognized by believers and secular psychologists alike, if it is true that there are two or more worldviews and associated life options, that it is rational to adhere to, and that it violates no doxastic obligations to adhere to, then it is possible to hesitate between them conscientiously as well as willfully. To deny this is to deny that it is possible to adhere to a position other than one's own without violating doxastic obligations. To show this, one needs to do much more than prove that there are phenomena that bespeak the truth of one's own faith to those who have it. It is necessary to show that those who read those phenomena differently, or even doubt their reality, are guilty of some form of irrationality. This is to deny that the world is ambiguous after all.

The boot in this controversy is in fact on the other foot. If the world really is ambiguous, there are some faiths for which this is a *problem.* Put simply, how can it be that a God who wishes us to respond to him reveals his reality only in ways that it is possible conscientiously not to recognize? If one or more of the theistic faiths is true, why is it not *unambiguously* true? This problem may well have adequate answers within those traditions where it can arise, but it is not an inconsiderable one, especially if the advocate of such a tradition rejects appeals to evidence or any other form of natural theology.[24]

2. One answer sometimes given to this latter question also suggests itself as a response to the ambiguity of the world: This ambiguity is necessary for our freedom to be preserved. Since the great postaxial faiths demand so much from those they speak to, it must be possible for these demands to be accepted or rejected freely. But if the truth of the faith were obvious, such freedom would not exist, and we would all be unable to help believing. Hence the signs of the truth that exist must be ambiguous ones that it is possible to interpret in other ways.

This view is, in the first place, incompatible with the claim of Paul and Calvin that God fills the world with unmistakable signs of his presence. One cannot say both that God's reality is unmistakably shown to us and that he leaves only ambiguous signs of it. But if someone maintains, as it seems Kierkegaard does in *Philosophical Fragments,* that God has to appear in disguise for our freedom to be preserved, the answer is that such a view confuses showing us something with shattering us into submission. Some of the most famous and crucial examples of reported encounters with the presence of God are overwhelming events, such as the visions of Isaiah or Ezekiel or Paul's conversion experience on the road to Damascus. But it is mere confusion to suppose that having the truth made clear to us would have to take such forms. To have the truth made clear is to have it placed beyond reasonable doubt. This could come about through a cogent philosophical demonstration of the sort that Aquinas tried to provide in the Five Ways or through some action or event that could not be reasonably accounted for except for the truth of the claim it is said to support, such as the alleged miracles of the New Testament. These need not be overwhelming; philosophical arguments never are, and miracles need not be dramatic. For those who hear and witness them can refuse to agree that they show what they clearly do show. They can find flaws in the argument that they missed the first three times they heard it; and they can ascribe Lazarus's revival to psychokinesis rather than the power of God. These are foolish and pigheaded responses; they represent gross violations of doxastic responsibility. But we all have the freedom to respond like that in the face of the clearest truth. Doubts of this sort in the face of such evidence are blameworthy. But doubts in the face of *ambiguous* evidences are not. It is this that their ambiguity consists in.

In discussing the specious charms of radical fideism, I have maintained that the core of rationality consists in the determination, not to disguise doxastic conflict, but to resolve it. I submit now that the fact of our world's ambiguity is also a fact that we should not disguise from ourselves but rather seek as far as possible to remove. We have a doxastic duty to disambiguate our world if we can. The attempt to discharge this duty is a task for philosophers.

I pointed out previously that if any of the arguments of classical natural theology were successful, we would not, after all, live in an ambiguous world, for it would have been proved that the world is the creation of God. This would prove the falsity of naturalism and of those religious forms, such as Buddhism, that are inconsistent with theism. As the practitioners of natural theology have all realized, this would not show that (say) any particular form of Christian teaching is true, as distinct from other forms of Christianity, or from Judaism and Islam; for this, further forms of appeal to experience or argument would be necessary. But a huge step toward disambiguating our world would have been taken. And it would not be taken at the price of embracing any form of Enlightenment foundationalism.

What would such a partial disambiguation of our world achieve? To answer this, we must consider, first, what is involved in proving something. It is not possible for me to repeat arguments I have used elsewhere, but I have followed the lead of George Mavrodes in seeing proof as "person-relative."[25] Proving is something one person does to another, beginning with premises that state truths the hearer knows. If the hearer does not know these truths, then no proof that depends on them is possible for that hearer. What can be proved to me is a function in part of what I know and what I understand and in part of my capacity to follow arguments. I have argued elsewhere that we have a proof when we have a true conclusion in an argument that begins with premises that are true and are known by the hearer of the argument to be true, which can be stated without stating the conclusion and which either entail it or make it overwhelmingly probable. It is clearly also necessary that the hearer understand that the premises support the conclusion in one of these two ways. For the most part the arguments of traditional natural theology have another feature additional to these: The premises from which they start are premises that are selected because they are obvious to everyone. This feature, however, does not seem to be a necessary feature of all proofs and indeed is not a feature of the Ontological Proof.

Let us suppose I have had God's existence proved to me, although I have never believed in God before and have made naturalistic assumptions in all my thinking hitherto. (The same points that I am about to try making could be made on the assumption that I have had God's existence disproved when I have assumed his reality all through my life before this.) Such a conclusion will obviously have a disruptive effect on many other beliefs that I have; in Plantinga's language, it is something that runs counter to beliefs that lie deep in my noetic structure. Because of this, I would be not only a surprising person but also a frivolous and irrational one if I did not hesitate to accept the conclusion without the most careful reflection. I should properly want to be sure of the logic of the argument; I should properly want to be sure that the premises of that argument are indeed true and that I have not neglected any doxastic obligations in agreeing to them. All such forms of resistance are right and proper. I might even reasonably put this conclusion to one side while I review all the beliefs I have that it would overturn, just because of the practical implications that accepting it would carry. But there is a limit to the propriety and the rationality of such hesitations; for if the proposition now before me is indeed proved to me, then it has been placed beyond reasonable doubt for me, and although I may have many entrenched beliefs that are inconsistent with it and do not go away because of its arrival, it is my doxastic duty as a rational being to resolve this conflict *in the proposition's favor.* If I do not accommodate it in this way, then I am guilty of ir-rationality or self-deception.

These are common phenomena; people are often irrational, and they deceive themselves continually. It is important to recognize that the disambiguation of the world can take place for me without my beliefs being changed. What has changed is the fact that it is no longer possible for me rationally to reject what has now been shown to be true or to go on believing what has been shown to be false. Our world can be disambiguated without anyone changing a single opinion. So the effect of disambiguating arguments lies in the rationality of the beliefs the hearers of such arguments have, which may or may not be reflected in different doxastic allegiances. If the disambiguating argument is not a proof, but merely one that shows its conclusion (such as the existence of God) to be likely or proba-ble (which is all that Swinburne claims for his theistic arguments, for example), then longer resistance and hesitation are manifestly reasonable, unless prudential considerations can properly be brought to bear.

There is a critical feature of traditional natural theology that has not so far formed part of our argument. In attempting to prove the existence of God, or to show it to be likely, natural theologians have always begun from truths that are recognized by both believ-ers and unbelievers. Although these have tended to be simple com-monsense truths, such as the reality of motion or the fact of biolog-ical adaptation, there is nothing in the nature of the probative enterprise that prevents its beginning from some quite recondite scientific discovery. What has been tacitly assumed to be essential has been the restriction of the premises to truths that one can recog-nize without already recognizing the existence of God: to what we may call nontheistic premises. There is nothing in the nature of proof itself that prevents us from proving a conclusion from premises that we could not know to be true without already know-ing that our conclusion was true. Producing a proof like that might have great value in, for example, showing us the relationship be-tween truths whose connections had not been as clear to us as they should be. But the forms of apologetic embodied in the arguments of traditional natural theology were not intended in this way. They had a different purpose: to show that unbelievers who accepted the premises could not, without irrationality, deny the existence of God since that was entailed by those premises or shown to be overwhelmingly probable by them. The arguments were intended to show the irrationality of continued unbelief by standards already accepted by the arguments' hearers. Someone seeking to disambiguate our world in the direction of theism would, following this model, have to begin with truths found within the shared secular scientific culture and show those who accept its beliefs and procedures that they have no rational choice but to accept God's existence also.

Disambiguation might be negative, not positive. It might be that someone could begin with some truths that our shared scientific culture enables us all to recognize and prove from this that God could not exist or that his existence is very unlikely. My present contention is that, although theism and naturalism (and their competitors) are rational views of the world, it is also incumbent on the rational inquirer who is aware of this fact to seek whatever degree of disambiguation is possible.

The proponents of the Basic Belief Apologetic may have shown that the foundationalist demand for external validation of theism does not have to be met before belief in God is rational. But the fact of our world's ambiguity shows that there is very good reason for hoping that such external validation is available. It shows that however we may feel ourselves to be emancipated from the demands of classical foundationalism, the need for a successful natural theology does not vanish with the advent of that heady freedom. For without natural theology there is no way beyond a situation in which adherents of opposed belief systems peer over their defenses at one another and explain one another away.

The key to disambiguation is the existence of the common scientific culture that believers and unbelievers share (and that, as the Basic Belief Apologetic emphasizes, they share without benefit of philosophical refutations of skepticism). One does not have to have a faith, or to be an unbeliever, to participate in that culture. Hence the criteria of assessment of any arguments within natural theology do not derive from assumptions of theism or atheism. If they did, then the use of such arguments would merely reinforce, and not cure, the ambiguity of the world.

What is true for natural theology is also true of what we might call, following an early work of Plantinga, natural atheology.[26] Critics of theism have often pointed to facts in the world that they think undermine, or defeat, belief in God, such as the depth and ex-

tent of evil. But these criticisms derive their power from the fact
that theists themselves emphasize the reality of evil more than atheists do and offer faith in God as the practical answer to it. So this
sort of atheological reasoning could be seen, and indeed often is
seen, as an attempt to reveal internal contradictions in the theist's
position. A natural atheology that began from some scientific fact
or theory would attempt to show that our shared world is one
whose nature precludes us from rationally ascribing its existence or
character to the creative power of a God. Such reasoning, if successful, would disambiguate our world in an atheist, or at least a non-
theist, direction.

Since I have emphasized that we live in a world that shows *multiple* ambiguity, and not merely theist-atheist ambiguity, it is necessary to add what the preceding argument makes obvious: The
search for disambiguation will also entail a search for a parallel
mode of decision between other competing religions and naturalisms. It might be thought that an argument that proved some
bedrock proposition of one tradition would serve to eliminate all
those incompatible with it, the obvious example being a proof of
the existence of God, which would a fortiori refute every religion
and naturalism that entailed atheism. This is, I think, true; though if
the hearer of such a proof had one of those systems deeply embedded in his or her epistemic structure, this would justify a very cau-
tious (though not an indefinite) scrutiny of that proof. In the absence of such a radical disambiguating success, one might have to be
content with the lesser but surely important achievement of refut-
ing some of the competitors with which one's own preferred system has to deal.

Some Examples

I now offer a few illustrations of ongoing debates that hold the
promise of furthering the process of disambiguating the world that
confronts the contemporary rational inquirer. I refrain from offering a view on any of the debates on which I report here and confine
myself to indicating what effect might be achieved if the argument
in question were pursued successfully. Each debate depends on assessing the implications of scientific developments in which I have
no firsthand competence, and all arguments that lean on such developments run the well-known risk of becoming obsolete, as many

think that (say) the arguments of Aquinas's natural theology have. If it should turn out that the scientific premises of some such argument are mistaken, then any degree of disambiguation achieved by that argument will only be apparent and not real.

1. I begin with some well-known contemporary attempts to use recent developments in cosmology for a revised Argument from Design. Older versions of this argument, such as that of Paley, tended to concentrate on observed facts of biological adaptation and to say that the adjustment of organisms to the challenges of their environments could not be accidental but had to be the outcome of prior planning on the part of a creator. Darwin seems to have undermined arguments of this form by offering an alternative way of understanding such adaptation. More recent versions of the Design Argument begin from the fact that the cosmos has shown the remarkable good sense of producing us and that it could not have done so if conditions in its remote past had been even modestly different from what they actually were. For example, if the initial rate of expansion at the time of the Big Bang had been one part in a million less than it was, there would have been a premature collapse before the elements could form, and if it had been one part in a million greater than it was, the stars and heavier elements could not have formed. Hence, it is said, the fact that carbon-based life has developed and intelligent living beings have evolved is the result of features in the initial development of the cosmos that are extremely unlikely to have been in place but for what is commonly called fine-tuning.

I am not competent to comment on the detail of this argument. But if one were to judge an argument of this form to be successful, then it would presumably show that intelligence is not only a product of cosmic development but also a creative factor within it. This does not amount to full-blooded theism, but it does eliminate wholly naturalistic worldviews and thus narrows the range of options among which the rational inquirer must choose. It would therefore serve as partial disambiguation of our world.[27]

2. A second argument worthy of mention here is presented by Richard Swinburne.[28] He contends that, although evolutionary biology can explain why natural selection has promoted the survival of organisms capable of intelligent behavior, it can do nothing to explain why beings who exhibit such adaptive behavior also have consciousness (feelings, thoughts, desires). There seems nothing

logically odd about the suggestion that the adaptive behavior that has survival value might take place without consciousness. He does not deny that consciousness requires great neural complexity to occur, but he does deny that this complexity explains why consciousness occurs at all. He holds that the only sort of explanation possible is in terms of a creative choice of consciousness as a good to be specially realized by creation. If this argument is successful, I judge it to show that the conscious experience that is given such central value and importance in all the religious traditions is anomalous on naturalistic worldviews—although it does not on the surface seem to be more readily explained by a theistic worldview than by a pantheistic or panentheistic one.[29] If arguments such as these two were judged successful, they would provide a basis for reflection on which of the non-naturalistic worldviews is the more likely. I turn now to arguments that are thought by their authors to undermine, not to support, particular religious positions.

3. The first is that of Richard Dawkins in his best-selling book *The Blind Watchmaker*.[30] He argues that the Darwinian theory of what he calls cumulative selection is not merely a naturalistic alternative that makes the hypothesis of design unnecessary but is also a theory that requires an appeal to a degree of chance that shows a design hypothesis to be false. If this argument is sound, then the doctrine of creation, or at least the doctrine of *purposeful* creation, becomes highly questionable on scientific grounds. Instead of the growth of scientific understanding making the belief in God seem inevitable, as it did to Paley, it now makes that belief seem at odds with what is known about the evolutionary process. (It is possible that a doctrine of creation as *lila*, that is, as nonpurposive, could survive the acceptance of an argument of this kind and might even be strengthened by it.[31])

4. My last example is taken from John Hick's *Death and Eternal Life*.[32] In one of the most interesting and well-argued parts of that work, Hick raises the question of whether the doctrine of karma, which is central to those religious traditions that teach rebirth, is compatible with the findings of modern genetics. My estimate of the case as he presents it is that his verdict of Not Proven is one that underestimates the difficulties of reconciling the two. Although at first sight the findings of genetics may seem to confirm the claims of the doctrine of karma regarding the built-in traits that determine so much of a person's life pattern, as soon as one enters into

specifics, the reverse appears to be true. For example, although the genetic inheritance of special abilities and character traits is a matter of genetic contributions transmitted through one's parents, one's karmic ancestors cannot include one's biological parents; and even though the doctrine of karma seems to entail the Lamarckian view of the inheritance of acquired characteristics, this position is wholly discredited in modern biology.

Faith and the Value of Arguments

Some may wonder how important the successful discovery of a mode of disambiguation would really be. Are there clearly many in the contemporary world who are in a spiritual predicament because of the ambiguity of that world? And are they to be rescued from that supposed predicament by *philosophers?*

The ambiguity of the world is a function of the ways in which it is reasonable for informed persons to interpret it rather than of the ways in which it *is* interpreted. The world can be ambiguous when all members of some group hold firmly to one reading of it when facts that reasonably suggest some other reading are accessible. So the fact that there are very many who are sure that a particular Christian, Islamic, Buddhist, or atheist interpretation is correct and can discern no merit in the competition does not show the world is not ambiguous, only that they do not recognize this.

The same would be true of some truth that disambiguated it. People continually persevere in holding on to received wisdoms that have been disproved and in pouring scorn on proved facts. But if they do, it is their own fault; they are not fulfilling their doxastic obligations. Disambiguating truths might well not produce any discernible spiritual or doxastic changes. But if they did not, it would be because of laziness or obstinacy or self-deception. The great religions of the world tell us that these are the causes that stand in the way of our salvation or liberation. Many naturalists say that these same causes generate religious belief and deflect believers from realistic engagement with their actual needs. Even though human beings are prone to laziness, obstinacy, or self-deception, neither of these opposed claims can be made out if the world really is an ambiguous one; for such a world gives us good reason to hesitate in the face of what religion and naturalism both tell us. But if the world is disambiguated, one of these claims would be true. It would not be possible to follow our doxastic obligations and hold back.

I have maintained that the disambiguation of the world is a philosophical task. Why this particular emphasis on *argument?* It might seem that someone's world could be disambiguated by encountering a spiritual leader, experiencing the closeness of God in nature or at a friend's deathbed, or (alternatively) suddenly experiencing the overwhelming sense of the world's meaninglessness and emptiness that so characterized the drama of the middle years of our century. But if someone is converted to a faith or driven to apostasy by some crucial spiritual experience, though he or she has certainly made up his or her mind in one way and has ceased to hesitate, and although it is altogether rational to do this and even prudentially unwise to go on hesitating, it may still be rational to have taken a contrary decision. Similarly, as Alston argues in response to the fact of religious ambiguity, it is perfectly right and doxastically proper to continue in one's present faith in response to the fact of the world's ambiguity;[33] but the same can be said, in such a world, of one's competitors. But none of this would obtain if the world were disambiguated by argument.

As we have seen already in other connections, we cannot all wait for the philosophers to determine which of the arguments they fight over is a sound one before we make our life-forming decisions. It is not only religious beliefs that we have to commit ourselves on without waiting for philosophers. But an ambiguous world is one in which it is rational to go on holding a preferred worldview and also rational to hold many others and *in which the informed thinker knows this.* I have suggested that this fact has a quite reasonably inhibiting effect on the faith one may have. Although one may, and perhaps must, continue *in* that faith even though one is fully cognizant of the alternatives, because life must go on, the fullness of that faith is likely to be somewhat diluted. I conclude, therefore, with two comments on the way in which the person who has a religious faith should consider the proper role of philosophical reflection.

First, what committed but intellectually responsible adherents of a faith should do is try their best to find disambiguating arguments in favor of the faith they live by. That is what Aquinas and the other great natural theologians tried to do in respect of Christianity, and the topical value of the enterprise has not diminished. Adherents should also take a lead from these great predecessors and recognize that not all the potential disambiguators will come from natural science and philosophy. It is possible that some will come from history. Most academic believers, for example, respond with embarrassment to phenomena such as the Turin Shroud or the supposed discovery of the remains of the Ark on Mount Ararat. I share their tastes but resist their conclusions: Such phenomena might provide the major or minor premises for arguments that go some way to entrench the teachings of the faith they are being used to further. One cannot rule this possibility out in advance for purely aesthetic reasons.

Some suppose that it would prostitute philosophy to be used in this way. But it is rare to find a philosopher who has no preferences about how the argument he or she constructs will turn out. What philosophers have to be judged by is the quality of the arguments they produce. Philosophically competent believers should do what the great apologists have tried to do: produce disambiguating arguments. They should not, above all, interpret the real successes of the Basic Belief Apologetic as demonstrating that their absence, or the ambiguity of the world, are to be welcomed.

Second, although it is quite consistent with intellectual integrity to look for arguments to justify where one is already, this integrity also demands that one not be indifferent to the outcome of the attempt to find them. If one tries and fails and the result is the prolongation of the ambiguity, then even though this may make the faith one has more tentative and less unhesitating, this may merely be the price one has to pay for maintaining faith and integrity together in a pluralistic age.

Notes

1. Hick 1989, Part 2.
2. Ibid., 73.
3. Penelhum 1971b, Chapter 15.
4. See Chapter 4.
5. See the conclusion of the previous chapter. For an enlightening discussion of an important Islamic parallel to the view of Paul and Calvin, see Part 2 of Akhtar 1990.
6. Hume 1957.
7. Paley 1838, vol. 2, 1.

8. Hick 1989, Chapter 2.

9. Smart 1958; Stace 1960; Zaehner 1957, 1970; Stoeber 1992, 1993, 1994. I pass over here the related question of how far it is possible to distinguish the experience of the mystic from the doctrinal interpretation of it found in that mystic's belief system. Katz 1978. Alston is wholly clear about the way in which his use of "mystical" differs from that of Stace; see Alston 1991, 23–25.

10. Annas and Barnes 1985, 151.

11. Hick 1989; Sharma 1993.

12. Hick 1989, 236.

13. Smith 1977, 1979.

14. "Indeed one might perhaps sum up one aspect of the history of these matters over the past few centuries in the following way. The affirmation 'I believe in God' used to mean: 'Given the reality of God as a fact of the universe, I hereby pledge to Him my heart and soul. I committedly opt to live in loyalty to Him. I offer my life to be judged by Him, trusting His mercy.' Today the statement may be taken by some as meaning: 'Given the uncertainty as to whether there be a God or not, as a fact of modern life, I announce that my opinion is "yes." I judge God to be existent.'" Smith 1977, 44.

15. Smith 1979, 141.

16. Ibid., 166.

17. Hatch 1957, 137–138.

18. Plantinga 1983a, 81.

19. Moore 1959, 33.

20. Smith 1979, 30.

21. See ibid., 84.

22. See Bertrand Russell's famous essay "A Free Man's Worship," Penelhum 1989.

23. Penelhum 1983, 1992b; Hallie 1966.

24. On this question, see Schellenberg 1993.

25. Mavrodes 1970, Part 2; Penelhum 1971a, Chapter 2, 1983, Chapter 5.

26. Plantinga 1967.

27. Leslie 1989, 1990.

28. Swinburne 1986.

29. Panentheism identifies the divine principle with some part or power within the universe rather than with the whole of it.

30. Dawkins 1986.

31. Lipner 1986, 381–388.

32. Hick 1976, 381–388.

33. Alston 1991, Chapter 7.

APPENDIX: READING
SUGGESTIONS

The purpose of this appendix is to provide some pointers to further reading on the topics examined in this book. There is no attempt at completeness. Works marked with the entry (B) contain valuable bibliographies on their themes. Full details on the books and articles listed here are to be found in the Bibliography.

General Works

There are a large number of general introductions to the philosophy of religion. Good examples are John Hick, *Philosophy of Religion* (1963); Thomas McPherson, *The Philosophy of Religion* (1965); and Vincent Brümmer, *Theology and Philosophical Inquiry* (1981) (the last is aimed particularly at theology students). Most such works concentrate on the traditional proofs of God and on the conceptual problems that dominated analytical debate about religion from midcentury until about 1980. They are complemented by a large number of anthologies that occasionally widen the area of debate. Among the best ones are Basil Mitchell (ed.), *The Philosophy of Religion* (1971); Baruch A. Brody (ed.), *Readings in the Philosophy of Religion* (1992); and Daniel Kolak and Raymond Martin (eds.), *Self, Cosmos, God* (1993).

There are a comparably large number of books on the academic study of religion. General descriptive accounts that help reveal the variety of methods scholars use to understand the phenomena of the religious life include such works as Frederick J. Streng, *Understanding Religious Life* (1984); and Jan de Vries, *The Study of Religion: A Historical Approach* (1967). Some particularly famous works are Mircea Eliade, *The Sacred and the Profane* (1957); Peter Berger, *The Sacred Canopy* (1969); and Wilfred Cantwell Smith, *The Meaning and End of Religion* (1962). The writings of Ninian Smart are noteworthy for the way in which he connects the concerns of the "phenomenological" students of religion with those of philosophers. His 1973 study, *The Phenomenon of Religion*, is particularly directed to this theme.

There are many texts devoted to comparative description of the religions of the world. One of the best known and most readable is Huston Smith, *The Religions of Man* (1958), now reissued as *The World's Religions* (1991). Readers might also consult John A. Hutchison, *Paths of Faith* (1969); or Ninian Smart, *The World's Religions* (1989).

The Nature of Faith

The most important recent studies of the nature of faith are John Hick, *Faith and Knowledge* (1966); and Richard Swinburne, *Faith and Reason* (1981). Hick's entry "Faith," in Paul Edwards (ed.), *Encyclopedia of Philosophy* (1967), is also valuable (B). The anthology *Faith* (1989), edited by Terence Penelhum, attempts to represent a wide variety of competing understandings (B).

A basic Christian source is the long article by Rudolf Bultmann and A. Weiser on *pistis* in Gerhard Kittel and Gerhard Friedrich (eds.), *Theological Dictionary of the New Testament* (1968). A typical contemporary Protestant study is Gerhard Ebeling, *The Nature of Faith* (1966). An important, though difficult, Jewish treatment is Martin Buber, *Two Types of Faith* (1961). Although there is no entry "Faith" in the *Encyclopedia Judaica*, there is a short one in Goeffrey Wigoder, *The Encyclopedia of Judaism* (1989). There are also valuable incidental comments in Solomon Schechter, *Aspects of Rabbinic Theology* (1961); and I have found helpful the title essay in Norman Lamm, *Faith and Doubt: Studies in Traditional Jewish Thought* (1971). A most valuable scholarly examination of key religious concepts, including that of faith, in Islam is Toshihiko Izutsu, *Ethico-Religious Concepts in the Qur'än* (1966); a very accessible discussion by an Islamic philosopher is Shabbir Akhtar, *A Faith for All Seasons* (1990).

Faith and Western Philosophy

On the evolution from religion to philosophy among the Greeks, standard works are F. M. Cornford, *From Religion to Philosophy: A Study in the Origins of Western Speculation* (1957); and Henri Frankfort et al., *Before Philosophy: The Intellectual Adventure of Ancient Man* (1949). On the interaction between Christianity and classical culture, see particularly Edwin Hatch, *The Influence of Greek Ideas on Christianity* (1957) (B); and Charles Norris Cochrane, *Christianity and Classical Culture* (1940).

On the faith and reason debates in medieval times, see Etienne Gilson, *Reason and Revelation in the Middle Ages* (1938). There is a helpful short account of Augustine's views on faith in Chapter 3 of Louis P. Pojman, *Religious Belief and the Will* (1986).

On the vast and indefinitely rewarding study of Aquinas, the reader is recommended to consult Norman Kretzmann and Eleonore Stump (eds.), *The Cambridge Companion to Aquinas* (1992). I am myself indebted to Philip H. Wicksteed, *The Reaction Between Dogma and Philosophy, Illustrated from the Works of St. Thomas Aquinas* (1920). An intellectually vigorous contemporary Thomist is E. L. Mascall; see, for example, his *Existence and Analogy* (1949). The important topic of analogy in Thomas's system is one that I have had to pass by here; an erudite treatment of it is to be found in J. F. Ross, *Portraying Analogy* (1981).

The nature and influence of classical Skepticism are still far less well known that they should be. Good introductions to them are Julia Annas and Jonathan Barnes, *The Modes of Scepticism: Ancient Texts and Modern Interpretations* (1985); and Myles Burnyeat (ed.), *The Skeptical Tradition* (1983). Annas and Barnes have recently produced a new translation of Sextus Empiricus, *Outlines of Scepticism* (1994). Richard Popkin, *The History of Scepticism from Erasmus to Spinoza* (1979), is indispensable for an understanding of the impact of the Pyrrhonian tradition on early modern thought. The best-known early modern skeptic is Montaigne, on whom there is a sympathetic study by Philip P. Hallie, *The Scar of Montaigne: An Essay in Personal Philosophy* (1966).

There is a large literature on Descartes. Serious students must consult Anthony Kenny, *Descartes* (1968); E. M. Curley *Descartes Against the Skeptics* (1978); and Bernard Williams, *Descartes: The Project of Pure Enquiry* (1978).

With Pascal there is no substitute for the *Pensées* themselves. The Alban J. Krailsheimer translation is recommended. Helpful guides are to be found in Alban Krailsheimer, *Pascal* (1980); Roger Hazelton, *Blaise Pascal: The Genius of His Thought* (1974); and Thomas V. Morris, *Making Sense of It All: Pascal and the Meaning of Life* (1992).

The standard work on Hume's philosophy of religion is John C.A. Gaskin, *Hume's Philosophy of Religion* (1988); also recommended is Keith E. Yandell, *Hume's "Inexplicable Mystery": His Views on Religion* (1990). On Kant's philosophy of religion, the reader might try C.C.J. Webb, *Kant's Philosophy of Religion* (1926); or Allen W. Wood, *Kant's Moral Religion* (1970).

For studies of Kierkegaard, see Heywood Thomas, *Subjectivity and Paradox* (1957); Louis J. Pojman, *The Logic of Subjectivity: Kierkegaard's Philosophy of Religion* (1984); and M. Jamie Ferreira, *Transforming Vision: Imagination and Will in Kierkegaardian Faith* (1991). I have attempted some analysis of my own in *God and Skepticism* (1983).

The best general work on Wittgenstein is probably Anthony Kenny, *Wittgenstein* (1973). There are some rather meager notes on his views about religion in *Wittgenstein: Lectures and Conversations on Aesthetic,*

Psychology, and Religious Belief (1966), edited by Cyril Barrett. Alan Keightley, *Wittgenstein, Grammar, and God* (1976), is helpful. The work of D. Z. Phillips, which I have not been able to discuss in this book, is best studied in his books *The Concept of Prayer* (1965), *Faith and Philosophical Enquiry* (1970), and *Faith After Foundationalism* (1988).

The Theistic Proofs

The literature on the proofs of the existence of God is very large. John Hick and Arthur C. McGill have a valuable anthology of literature on the Ontological Proof, called *The Many-Faced Argument* (1967) (B). Its most recent formulation is in Alvin Plantinga, *The Nature of Necessity* (1974). There is a new translation of Anselm's original version, with commentary, in Gregory Schufreider, *Confessions of a Rational Mystic* (1994). For the Cosmological and Design Arguments, see Anthony Kenny, *The Five Ways* (1969); William L. Rowe, *The Cosmological Argument* (1975); and Hugo Meynell, *The Intelligible Universe* (1982). More severely critical treatments are John L. Mackie, *The Miracle of Theism* (1982); and Richard M. Gale, *On the Nature and Existence of God* (1991). The most substantial contribution to natural theology in our time is undoubtedly that of Richard Swinburne, *The Existence of God* (1979).

Belief and the Will

The classic examination of belief is H. H. Price, *Belief* (1969). An important recent discussion of belief and will is Louis J. Pojman, *Religious Belief and the Will* (1986).

Faith and Rationality

There has been a substantial growth in philosophical discussion of the emotions in recent years. Readers might consult William Lyons, *Emotion* (1980); and Amélie Rorty (ed.), *Explaining Emotions* (1980) (B).

On the classical prudential arguments for belief in God, see Nicholas Rescher, *Pascal's Wager: A Study of Practical Reasoning in Philosophical Theology* (1985) (B); Terence Penelhum, *Butler* (1985); and James C.S. Wernham, *James's Will-to-Believe Doctrine: A Heretical View* (1987) (B).

On the Basic Belief Apologetic, William Alston, *Perceiving God: The Epistemology of Religious Experience* (1991), stands out. The fullest statement of Alvin Plantinga's position prior to the recent publication of the first two volumes of his projected trilogy has been the essay "Reason and Belief in God" (1983a); the first two volumes of the trilogy itself, *Warrant:*

The Current Debate and *Warrant and Proper Function,* appeared together in 1993. The essays by Nicholas Wolterstorff that are listed in the bibliography are also of considerable importance. The reader should also consult Kelly J. Clark, *Return to Reason: A Critique of Enlightenment Evidentialism and a Defense of Reason and Belief in God* (1990). Serious critiques of the apologetic are not yet available, although the interested reader could well consult Linda Zagzebski (ed.), *Rational Faith: Catholic Responses to Reformed Epistemology* (1983).

Faith and Ambiguity

John Hick's analysis of the religious ambiguity of the world is to be found in Part Two of *An Interpretation of Religion: Human Responses to the Transcendent* (1989). My own former understanding of this ambiguity, summarized in this book, was originally presented in *Religion and Rationality* (1971b), Chapter 15; and in the essay "Is a Religious Epistemology Possible?" (1970). See also Stewart R. Sutherland, *Faith and Ambiguity* (1984). For a deeply pessimistic view of the implications of ambiguity for theism, see John L. Schellenberg, *Divine Hiddenness and Human Reason* (1993).

The implications of religious pluralism are central to all of Hick's recent writings. Some useful discussion of his views is to be found in Arvind Sharma (ed.), *God, Truth, and Reality: Essays in Honour of John Hick* (1993). The views of Wilfred Cantwell Smith that have been discussed here are to be found in the three works *Belief and History* (1977), *Faith and Belief* (1979), and *Towards a World Theology* (1981). From the time of *Reasons and Faiths* (1958) onward, Ninian Smart's work has continually reminded philosophers and students of religion of the comparative issues to which the theories of Hick and Smith are responses. The implications of religious pluralism have been of special concern to Christian thinkers because of the Christian insistence on the uniqueness of Christ. For some examples of Christian thought on this subject, see John Hick and Brian Hebblethwaite (eds.), *Christianity and Other Religions* (1980) (B).

The debates whose resolution might provide disambiguating conclusions are all debates to which a large literature is relevant. Recent cosmological versions of the Design Argument are splendidly discussed in John Leslie, *Universes* (1989); and the same author's anthology *Physical Cosmology and Philosophy* (1990) (B) provides excellent ancillary and background material. A vigorous theistic argument of this type is to be found in M. A. Corey, *God and the New Cosmology: The Anthropic Design Argument* (1993) (B). Arguments such as those offered (in opposite directions) by Swinburne and Dawkins need to be assessed in the light of an understanding of the limits of biological explanation. A good beginning here for philosophical readers is the anthology *The Philosophy of Biology*, edited by Michael Ruse (1989). Richard Swinburne's argument is to be found in *The Evolution of the Soul* (1986); Richard Dawkins's in *The Blind Watchmaker* (1986). I am aware of no direct reply to Hick's criticism of the doctrine of karma in *Death and Eternal Life* (1976); but there is much continuing discussion of the nature of that teaching, to which any assessment of his criticisms would have to pay attention. On this, see, for just one example, Ronald W. Neufeldt (ed.), *Karma and Rebirth: Post-Classical Developments* (1986).

Revelation

I have argued that religious faith is to be understood as a response to what is taken to be revelation; but this book contains no discussion of this vital notion. There have been two important, and different, philosophical explorations of it recently: George I. Mavrodes, *Revelation in Religious Belief* (1988); and Richard Swinburne, *Revelation: From Metaphor to Analogy* (1992). Future thought on the subject is bound to be much affected by the reflections in Wilfred Cantwell Smith, *What Is Scripture?: A Comparative Approach* (1993).

BIBLIOGRAPHY

Akhtar, Shabbir. 1990. *A Faith for All Seasons.* Chicago: Ivan R. Dee.
———. 1990. *The Light in the Enlightenment.* London: Grey Seal.
Alston, William P. 1991. *Perceiving God: The Epistemology of Religious Experience.* Ithaca: Cornell University Press.
Annas, Julia, and Jonathan Barnes. 1985. *The Modes of Scepticism: Ancient Texts and Modern Interpretations.* Cambridge: Cambridge University Press.
Anselm, Saint. 1903. *Proslogion.* Trans. S. N. Deane. La Salle, Ill.: Open Court.
Aquinas, Saint Thomas. 1952. *On Truth.* Trans. James V. McGlynn. Vol. 2. Chicago: Regnery.
———. 1955. *Summa Contra Gentiles.* Trans. as *On the Truth of the Catholic Faith.* Garden City, N.Y.: Doubleday.
———. 1974 and 1975. *Summa Theologiae, Secunda Secundae* (Part Two of Part Two), Questions 1–16. Latin text with English translation. Vols. 31 and 32. London: Eyre and Spottiswoode, Blackfriars Edition.
Augustine, Saint. 1943. *Against the Academicians.* Trans. Sister Mary Patricia Garvey. Milwaukee: Marquette University Press.
Barr, James. 1993. *Biblical Faith and Natural Theology.* Oxford: Clarendon Press.
Bayle, Pierre. 1734–1741. *A General Dictionary, Historical and Critical.* Trans. John Peter Bernard et al. London: James Bettenham.
———. 1965. *Historical and Critical Dictionary (Selections).* Trans. Richard H. Popkin. Indianapolis: Bobbs-Merrill.
Berger, Peter. 1969. *The Sacred Canopy.* Garden City, N.Y.: Doubleday.
Brody, Baruch A. (ed.). 1992. *Readings in the Philosophy of Religion.* 2d ed. Englewood Cliffs, N.J.: Prentice-Hall.
Brümmer, Vincent. 1981. *Theology and Philosophical Inquiry.* London: Macmillan.
Buber, Martin. 1961. *Two Types of Faith.* Trans. Norman P. Goldhawk. New York: Harper.
———. 1977. *The Prophetic Faith.* New York: Macmillan.
Bultmann, Rudolf, and Artur Weiser. 1968. "Pistis." In Gerhard Kittel and Gerhard Friedrich (eds.), *Theological Dictionary of the New Testament.* Grand Rapids, Mich.: Eerdmans.

Burnyeat, Myles. 1982. "Idealism and Greek Philosophy: What Descartes Saw and Berkeley Missed." *Philosophical Review* 91:3–40.

———. (ed.). 1983. *The Skeptical Tradition.* Berkeley and Los Angeles: University of California Press.

Butler, Joseph. 1900. *The Works of Joseph Butler.* Ed. J. H. Bernard. Vol. 2. London: Macmillan.

Byrne, Peter. 1989. *Natural Religion and the Nature of Religion: The Legacy of Deism.* London: Routledge.

Calvin, John. 1960. *Institutes of the Christian Religion* (1536). Trans. Ford L. Battles. 2 vols. Philadelphia: Westminster Press.

Clark, Kelly J. 1990. *Return to Reason: A Critique of Enlightenment Evidentialism and a Defense of Reason and Belief in God.* Grand Rapids, Mich.: Eerdmans.

Clarke, Samuel. 1978. *A Demonstration of the Being and Attributes of God* (Boyle Lectures 1704). In Vol. 2 of *The Works of Samuel Clarke.* 4 vols. London: Paul Knapton, 1738. Facsimile reprint, New York: Garland Publishing.

Cochrane, Charles Norris. 1940. *Christianity and Classical Culture.* Oxford: Clarendon Press.

Corey, M. A. 1993. *God and the New Cosmology: The Anthropic Design Argument.* Lanham, Md.: Rowman and Littlefield.

Cornford, Francis M. 1957. *From Religion to Philosophy: A Study in the Origins of Western Speculation.* New York: Harper.

Curley, Edwin M. 1978. *Descartes Against the Skeptics.* Oxford: Blackwell.

Danto, Arthur. 1973. *Analytical Philosophy of Action.* Cambridge: Cambridge University Press.

Dawkins, Richard. 1986. *The Blind Watchmaker.* London: Longman.

De Santillana, Giorgio. 1955. *The Crime of Galileo.* Chicago: University of Chicago Press.

De Vries, Jan. 1967. *The Study of Religion: A Historical Approach.* Trans. Kees W. Bolle. New York: Harcourt, Brace and World.

Descartes, René. 1966. *Philosophical Writings.* Trans. Elizabeth Anscombe and Peter Thomas Geach. London: Nelson.

Diogenes Laertius. 1853. *The Lives and Opinions of Eminent Philosophers.* Trans. C. D. Yonge. London: Bohn.

Ebeling, Gerhard. 1966. *The Nature of Faith.* Trans. Ronald Gregor Smith. London: Collins.

Eliade, Mircea. 1957. *The Sacred and the Profane.* New York: Harcourt.

Ferreira, M. Jamie. 1991. *Transforming Vision: Imagination and Will in Kierkegaardian Faith.* Oxford: Clarendon Press.

Fingarette, Herbert. 1969. *Self-Deception.* London: Routledge and Kegan Paul.

Flew, Antony G.N. 1976. *The Presumption of Atheism.* London: Paul Elek.

Flew, Antony, and Alasdair MacIntyre (eds.). 1955. *New Essays in Philosophical Theology.* London: SCM Press.

Frankfort, Henri, et al. 1949. *Before Philosophy: The Intellectual Adventure of Ancient Man.* Harmondsworth: Penguin.

Frankfurt, Harry G. 1988. "Freedom of the Will and the Concept of a Person." In Harry G. Frankfurt, *The Importance of What We Care About.* Cambridge: Cambridge University Press.

Gale, Richard M. 1991. *On the Nature and Existence of God.* Cambridge: Cambridge University Press.

Gaskin, John C.A. 1988. *Hume's Philosophy of Religion.* 2d ed. London: Macmillan.

Gilson, Etienne. 1938. *Reason and Revelation in the Middle Ages.* New York: Charles Scribner's Sons.

———. 1941. *God and Philosophy.* New Haven: Yale University Press.

Groarke, Leo. 1990. *Greek Scepticism: Anti-Realist Trends in Ancient Thought.* Montreal: McGill-Queen's University Press.

Hallie, Philip P. 1966. *The Scar of Montaigne: An Essay in Personal Philosophy.* Middletown, Conn.: Wesleyan University Press.

Hatch, Edwin. 1957. *The Influence of Greek Ideas on Christianity.* New York: Harper.

Hazelton, Roger. 1974. *Blaise Pascal: The Genius of His Thought.* Philadelphia: Westminster Press.

Heath, Peter (ed.). 1974. *The Philosopher's Alice.* New York: St. Martin's Press.

Hick, John. 1963. *Philosophy of Religion.* Englewood Cliffs, N.J.: Prentice-Hall.

———. 1966. *Faith and Knowledge.* 2d ed. Ithaca: Cornell University Press.

———. 1967. "Faith." In Paul Edwards (ed.), *Encyclopedia of Philosophy.* Vol. 3. New York: Macmillan–Free Press.

———. 1976. *Death and Eternal Life.* London: Collins.

———. 1989. *An Interpretation of Religion: Human Responses to the Transcendent.* London: Macmillan.

Hick, John, and Brian Hebblethwaite (eds.). 1980. *Christianity and Other Religions.* London: Collins.

Hick, John, and Arthur C. McGill (eds.). 1967. *The Many-Faced Argument.* New York: Macmillan.

Hookway, Christopher. 1990. *Scepticism.* London: Routledge.

Hume, David. 1947. *Dialogues Concerning Natural Religion.* Ed. Norman Kemp Smith. Edinburgh: Thomas Nelson.

———. 1957. *The Natural History of Religion.* Ed. H. E. Root. London: Adam and Charles Black.

———. 1970. *Dialogues Concerning Natural Religion.* Ed. Nelson Pike. Indianapolis: Bobbs-Merrill.

———. 1975. *Enquiries: Concerning Human Understanding and Concerning the Principles of Morals.* Ed. L. A. Selby-Bigge. Rev. P. H. Nidditch. Oxford: Clarendon Press.

———. 1978. *A Treatise of Human Nature.* Ed. L. A. Selby-Bigge. Rev. P. H. Nidditch. Oxford: Clarendon Press.

———. 1993. *Dialogues and Natural History of Religion.* Ed. John C.A. Gaskin. Oxford: Oxford University Press.

Hurlbutt, Robert H. 1965. *Hume, Newton, and the Design Argument.* Lincoln: University of Nebraska Press.

Hutchison, John A. 1969. *Paths of Faith.* New York: McGraw-Hill.

Huxley, Aldous. 1956. *Do What You Will.* London: Chatto and Windus.

Izutsu, Toshihiko. 1966. *Ethico-Religious Concepts in the Qur'än.* Montreal: McGill University Press.

James, William. 1979. *The Will to Believe and Other Essays in Popular Philosophy.* Cambridge, Mass.: Harvard University Press.

Kant, Immanuel. 1950. *Critique of Pure Reason.* Trans. Norman Kemp Smith. London: Macmillan.

Katz, Steven T. 1978. "Language, Epistemology, and Mysticism." In Steven T. Katz (ed.), *Mysticism and Philosophical Analysis.* London: Sheldon Press.

Keightley, Alan. 1976. *Wittgenstein, Grammar, and God.* London: Epworth Press.

Kenny, Anthony. 1968. *Descartes.* New York: Random House.

———. 1969. *The Five Ways.* London: Routledge and Kegan Paul.

———. 1973. *Wittgenstein.* Harmondsworth: Penguin.

———. 1992. *What Is Faith? Essays in the Philosophy of Religion.* Oxford: Oxford University Press.

Kierkegaard, Søren. 1941a. *Concluding Unscientific Postscript.* Trans. David F. Swenson and Walter Lowrie. Princeton: Princeton University Press.

———. 1941b. *Fear and Trembling and the Sickness unto Death.* Trans. Walter Lowrie. Princeton: Princeton University Press.

———. 1985. *Philosophical Fragments and Johannes Climacus.* Trans. Howard V. and Edna H. Hong. Princeton: Princeton University Press.

Kirwan, Christopher. 1983. "Augustine Against the Skeptics." In Myles Burnyeat (ed.), *The Skeptical Tradition.* Berkeley and Los Angeles: University of California Press.

Kolak, Daniel, and Raymond Martin (eds.). 1993. *Self, Cosmos, God.* Fort Worth, Tex.: Harcourt Brace Jovanovich.

Krailsheimer, Alban. 1980. *Pascal.* Oxford: Oxford University Press.

Kretzmann, Norman, and Eleonore Stump (eds.). 1992. *The Cambridge Companion to Aquinas.* Cambridge: Cambridge University Press.

Labrousse, Elisabeth. 1983. *Bayle.* Trans. Denys Potts. Oxford: Oxford University Press.

Lamm, Norman. 1971. *Faith and Doubt: Studies in Traditional Jewish Thought.* New York: Ktav.

Leslie, John. 1989. *Universes.* London: Routledge.

———. (ed.) 1990. *Physical Cosmology and Philosophy.* New York: Macmillan.

Lipner, Julius L. 1986. *The Face of Truth.* London: Macmillan.

Locke, John. 1958. *The Reasonableness of Christianity.* Ed. Ian T. Ramsey. London: Adam and Charles Black.

———. 1959. *Essay Concerning Human Understanding.* Ed. Alexander C. Fraser. 2 vols. Oxford: Oxford University Press, 1894. Reprint, New York: Dover Press.

Luther, Martin. 1957. "The Freedom of a Christian." Trans. W. A. Lambert. Rev. Harold J. Grimm. In *Luther's Works.* Vol. 31. Philadelphia: Muhlenberg Press.

Lyons, William. 1980. *Emotion.* Cambridge: Cambridge University Press.

MacGregor, Geddes. 1958. *The Vatican Revolution.* London: Macmillan.

Mackie, John L. 1982. *The Miracle of Theism.* Oxford: Clarendon Press.

Marks, Brian. 1976. "Thought, Belief, and the Will: A Study of the Cartesian Account of Judgment." Ph.D. diss., University of Calgary.

Mascall, Eric L. 1949. *Existence and Analogy.* London: Longmans Green.

Mavrodes, George I. 1970. *Belief in God: A Study in the Epistemology of Religion.* New York: Random House.

———. 1988. *Revelation in Religious Belief.* Philadelphia: Temple University Press.

McPherson, Thomas. 1965. *The Philosophy of Religion.* London: Van Nostrand.

Meynell, Hugo. 1982. *The Intelligible Universe.* London: Macmillan.

Mitchell, Basil. 1973. *The Justification of Religious Belief.* London: Macmillan.

———. (ed.). 1971. *The Philosophy of Religion.* Oxford: Oxford University Press.

Moore, G. E. 1959. *Philosophical Papers.* London: George Allen and Unwin.

Morris, Thomas V. 1992. *Making Sense of It All: Pascal and the Meaning of Life.* Grand Rapids, Mich.: Eerdmans.

Murti, T. R. V. 1960. *The Central Philosophy of Buddhism: A Study of the Mādhyamika System.* 2d ed. London: Allen and Unwin.

Neufeldt, Ronald W. (ed.). 1986. *Karma and Rebirth: Post-Classical Developments.* Albany: State University of New York Press.

Newman, John Henry. 1970. *University Sermons.* Ed. D. M. MacKinnon and J. D. Holmes. London: S.P.C.K.

Nock, Arthur D. 1965. *Conversion.* Oxford: Oxford University Press.

Norton, David Fate (ed.). 1993. *The Cambridge Companion to Hume.* Cambridge: Cambridge University Press.

Paley, William. 1838. *The Works of William Paley D.D.* 4 vols. London: Longman.

Pascal, Blaise. 1966. *Pensées.* Trans. Alban J. Krailsheimer. Harmondsworth: Penguin.

Pelikan, Jaroslav. 1971. *The Christian Tradition: A History of the Development of Doctrine.* Vol. 1: *The Emergence of the Catholic Tradition, 100–600.* Chicago: University of Chicago Press.

Penelhum, Terence. 1964. "Pascal's Wager." *Journal of Religion* 44:201–209.

———. 1970. "Is a Religious Epistemology Possible?" In Godfrey N.A. Vesey (ed.), *Knowledge and Necessity.* London: Macmillan.

———. 1971a. *Problems of Religious Knowledge.* London: Macmillan.

———. 1971b. *Religion and Rationality.* New York: Random House.

———. 1979. "Human Nature and External Desires." *The Monist* 62:304–319.

———. 1983. *God and Skepticism.* Dordrecht: Reidel.

———. 1985. *Butler.* London: Routledge and Kegan Paul.

———. 1992a. "Butler and Human Ignorance." In Christopher Cunliffe (ed.), *Joseph Butler's Moral and Religious Thought: Tercentenary Essays.* Oxford: Clarendon Press.

———. 1992b. *David Hume: An Introduction to His Philosophical System.* West Lafayette, Ind.: Purdue University Press.

———. 1992c. "Parity Is Not Enough." In Marcus Hester (ed.), *Faith, Reason, and Skepticism.* Philadelphia: Temple University Press.

———. 1993. "Human Nature and Truth: Hume and Pascal." *Lumen* 12:45–64.

———. (ed.). 1989. *Faith.* New York: Macmillan.

Phillips, D. Z. 1965. *The Concept of Prayer.* London: Routledge and Kegan Paul.

———. 1970. *Faith and Philosophical Enquiry.* London: Routledge and Kegan Paul.

———. 1988. *Faith After Foundationalism.* London: Routledge.

———. (ed.). 1967. *Religion and Understanding.* Oxford: Blackwell.

Plantinga, Alvin. 1967. *God and Other Minds: A Study of the Rational Justification of Belief in God.* Ithaca: Cornell University Press.

———. 1974. *The Nature of Necessity.* Oxford: Clarendon Press.

———. 1979. "Is Belief in God Rational?" In C. F. Delaney (ed.), *Rationality and Religious Belief.* Notre Dame, Ind.: Notre Dame University Press.

———. 1981. "Is Belief in God Properly Basic?" *Nous* 15:41–51.

———. 1982. "Rationality and Religious Belief." In Steven M. Cahn and David Shatz (eds.), *Contemporary Philosophy of Religion.* New York: Oxford University Press.

————. 1983a. "Reason and Belief in God." In Alvin Plantinga and Nicholas Wolterstorff (eds.), *Faith and Rationality.* Notre Dame, Ind.: Notre Dame University Press.

————. 1983b. "The Reformed Objection to Natural Theology." In Hendrick Hart, Johan van der Hoeven, and Nicholas Wolterstorff (eds.), *Rationality in the Calvinian Tradition.* Lanham, Md.: University Press of America.

————. 1992. "Agustinian Christian Philosophy." *The Monist* 75:291–320.

————. 1993a. "A Christian Life Partly Lived." In Kelly James Clark (ed.), *Philosophers Who Believe.* Downers Grove, Ill.: InterVarsity Press.

————. 1993b. *Warrant and Proper Function.* New York: Oxford University Press.

————. 1993c. *Warrant: The Current Debate.* New York: Oxford University Press.

Plato. 1965. *Meno: Text and Criticism.* Ed. Alexander Sesonske and Noel Fleming. Belmont, Calif.: Wadsworth.

————. 1990. *The Theaetetus of Plato.* Ed. Myles Burnyeat. Trans. M. J. Levett, Indianapolis: Hackett.

Pojman, Louis J. 1984. *The Logic of Subjectivity: Kierkegaard's Philosophy of Religion.* University: University of Alabama Press.

————. 1986. *Religious Belief and the Will.* London: Routledge and Kegan Paul.

Popkin, Richard. 1979. *The History of Scepticism from Erasmus to Spinoza.* Berkeley and Los Angeles: University of California Press.

————. 1980. *The High Road to Pyrrhonism.* Ed. Richard Watson and James Force. San Diego: Austin Hill Press.

————. 1993. "The Role of Scepticism in Modern Philosophy Reconsidered." *Journal of the History of Philosophy* 31:501–517.

Price, H. H. 1969. *Belief.* London: Allen and Unwin.

Rescher, Nicholas. 1985. *Pascal's Wager: A Study of Practical Reasoning in Philosophical Theology.* Notre Dame, Ind.: University of Notre Dame Press.

Robinson, Richard. 1964. *An Atheist's Values.* Oxford: Clarendon Press.

Rorty, Amélie Oksenberg (ed.). 1980. *Explaining Emotions.* Berkeley and Los Angeles: University of California Press.

Ross, James F. 1981. *Portraying Analogy.* Cambridge: Cambridge University Press.

Rowe, William L. 1975. *The Cosmological Argument.* Princeton: Princeton University Press.

Ruse, Michael (ed.). 1989. *The Philosophy of Biology.* New York: Macmillan.

Schechter, Solomon. 1961. *Aspects of Rabbinic Theology.* Intr. Louis Finkelstein. New York: Schocken Books.

Schellenberg, John L. 1993. *Divine Hiddenness and Human Reason.* Ithaca: Cornell University Press.

Schufreider, Gregory. 1994. *Confessions of a Rational Mystic.* West Lafayette, Ind.: Purdue University Press.

Sextus Empiricus. 1933–1949. *Works.* Trans. R. G. Bury. 4 vols. Loeb Classical Library. Cambridge, Mass.: Harvard University Press.

———. 1994. *Outlines of Scepticism.* Trans. Julia Annas and Jonathan Barnes. Cambridge: Cambridge University Press.

Sharma, Arvind (ed.). 1993. *God, Truth, and Reality: Essays in Honour of John Hick.* London: Macmillan.

Smart, Ninian. 1958. *Reasons and Faiths.* London: Routledge and Kegan Paul.

———. 1973. *The Phenomenon of Religion.* London: Macmillan.

———. 1989. *The World's Religions.* Cambridge: Cambridge University Press.

Smith, Huston. 1991. *The World's Religions.* San Francisco: Harper.

Smith, Wilfred Cantwell. 1962. *The Meaning and End of Religion.* New York: Macmillan.

———. 1977. *Belief and History.* Charlottesville: University Press of Virginia.

———. 1979. *Faith and Belief.* Princeton: Princeton University Press.

———. 1981. *Towards a World Theology.* London: Macmillan.

———. 1993. *What Is Scripture? A Comparative Approach.* Minneapolis: Fortress.

Stace, W. T. 1960. *Mysticism and Philosophy.* London: Macmillan.

Stoeber, Michael. 1992. "Constructivist Epistemologies of Mysticism: A Critique and a Revision." *Religious Studies* 28:107–116.

———. 1993. "Introvertive Mystical Experiences: Monistic, Theistic, and Theo-Monistic." *Religious Studies* 29:169–184.

———. 1994. *Theo-Monistic Mysticism: A Hindu-Christian Comparison.* London: Macmillan.

Stough, Charlotte L. 1969. *Greek Skepticism: A Study in Epistemology.* Berkeley and Los Angeles: University of California Press.

Streng, Frederick J. 1984. *Understanding Religious Life.* Belmont, Calif.: Dickenson.

Stump, Eleonore. 1989. "Faith and Goodness." In Godfrey Vesey (ed.), *The Philosophy in Christianity.* Cambridge: Cambridge University Press.

Sutherland, Stewart R. 1984. *Faith and Ambiguity.* London: SCM Press.

Swinburne, Richard. 1979. *The Existence of God.* Oxford: Clarendon Press.

———. 1981. *Faith and Reason.* Oxford: Clarendon Press.

———. 1986. *The Evolution of the Soul.* Oxford: Clarendon Press.

———. 1992. *Revelation: From Metaphor to Analogy.* Oxford: Clarendon Press.

Thomas, Heywood J. 1957. *Subjectivity and Paradox.* Oxford: Blackwell.

Tindal, Matthew. 1978. *Christianity As Old As the Creation.* New York: Garland Publishers.

Toland, John. 1964. *Christianity Not Mysterious.* Ed. G. Gawlick. Stuttgart–Bad Cannstatt: Friedrich Frommann.

Vesey, Godfrey (ed.). 1970. *Knowledge and Necessity.* London: Macmillan.

———. 1989. *The Philosophy in Christianity.* Cambridge: Cambridge University Press.

Webb, C.C.J. 1926. *Kant's Philosophy of Religion.* Oxford: Clarendon Press.

———. 1929. *Pascal's Philosophy of Religion.* Oxford: Clarendon Press.

Wernham, James C.S. 1987. *James's Will-to-Believe Doctrine: A Heretical View.* Montreal: McGill-Queen's University Press.

Wicksteed, Philip H. 1920. *The Reaction Between Dogma and Philosophy, Illustrated from the Works of St. Thomas Aquinas.* London: Williams and Norgate.

Wigoder, Geoffrey (ed.). 1989. *The Encyclopedia of Judaism.* New York: Macmillan.

Williams, Bernard. 1973. *Problems of the Self.* Cambridge: Cambridge University Press.

———. 1978. *Descartes: The Project of Pure Enquiry.* Harmondsworth: Penguin.

Winch, Peter. 1967. "Understanding a Primitive Society." In D. Z. Phillips (ed.), *Religion and Understanding.* Oxford: Blackwell.

Wittgenstein, Ludwig. 1966. *Lectures and Conversations on Aesthetic, Psychology, and Religious Belief.* Ed. Cyril Barrett. Oxford: Blackwell.

———. 1969. *On Certainty.* Ed. G.E.M. Anscombe and G. H. von Wright. Trans. Denis Paul and G.E.M. Anscombe. Oxford: Blackwell.

Wolterstorff, Nicholas. 1983a. "Can Belief in God Be Rational if It Has No Foundations?" In Alvin Plantinga and Nicholas Wolterstorff (eds.), *Faith and Rationality.* Notre Dame, Ind.: University of Notre Dame Press.

———. 1983b. "Thomas Reid on Rationality." In Hendrick Hart, Johan van der Hoven, and Nicholas Wolterstorff (eds.), *Rationality in the Calvinian Tradition.* Lanham, Md: University Press of America.

———. 1986. "The Migration of the Theistic Arguments: From Natural Theology to Evidentialist Apologetics." In Robert Audi and William J. Wainright (eds.), *Rationality, Religious Belief, and Moral Commitment: New Essays in the Philosophy of Religion.* Ithaca: Cornell University Press.

Wood, Allen W. 1970. *Kant's Moral Religion.* Ithaca: Cornell University Press.

Yandell, Keith E. 1990. *Hume's "Inexplicable Mystery": His Views on Religion.* Philadelphia: Temple University Press.

Zaehner, R. C. 1957. *Mysticism, Sacred and Profane.* Oxford: Oxford University Press.

———. 1970. *Concordant Discord: The Interdependence of Faiths.* Oxford: Clarendon Press.

Zagzebski, Linda (ed.). 1983. *Rational Faith: Catholic Responses to Reformed Epistemology.* Notre Dame, Ind.: University of Notre Dame Press.

ABOUT THE BOOK
AND AUTHOR

The concerns of philosophy and of religion overlap to a considerable extent—each seeks, among other things, to develop an account of mankind's place in the universe. But their relationship has never been an easy one. Faith gives rise to philosophical puzzlement just as secular beliefs do, but it also generates special philosophical questions that secular beliefs do not.

This engaging text encourages students and other readers to grapple with these special questions of faith, to look at how they relate to other issues in philosophy and in the empirical study of religion. Equally accurate and insightful in its treatment of historical authors such as Aquinas and Pascal as it is in treatment of such contemporaries as Plantinga and Alston, *Reason and Religious Faith* is the most up-to-date and balanced introduction to these issues available. It marks an advance over earlier surveys in its recognition of religious pluralism and the relevance of non-Christian religious views. It is an ideal introduction to the issues of religious epistemology for students of both religious studies and philosophy.

Terence Penelhum is professor emeritus of religious studies at the University of Calgary. He is author of many books and articles on the history of philosophy and the philosophy of religion, including *Religion and Rationality, Problems of Religious Knowledge,* and *God and Skepticism.*

INDEX